RETIREMENT ISSUES, PLANS AND LIFESTYLES

PRIVATE PENSIONS, LUMP SUM OFFERS, AND SPONSOR DE-RISKING

IMPLICATIONS AND ANALYSIS

Retirement Issues, Plans and Lifestyles

Additional books in this series can be found on Nova's website under the Series tab.

Additional e-books in this series can be found on Nova's website under the e-book tab.

RETIREMENT ISSUES, PLANS AND LIFESTYLES

PRIVATE PENSIONS, LUMP SUM OFFERS, AND SPONSOR DE-RISKING

IMPLICATIONS AND ANALYSIS

JAMES G. HUGHES
EDITOR

nova publishers
New York

NOTICE TO THE READER

The Publisher has taken reasonable care in the preparation of this book, but makes no expressed or implied warranty of any kind and assumes no responsibility for any errors or omissions. No liability is assumed for incidental or consequential damages in connection with or arising out of information contained in this book. The Publisher shall not be liable for any special, consequential, or exemplary damages resulting, in whole or in part, from the readers' use of, or reliance upon, this material. Any parts of this book based on government reports are so indicated and copyright is claimed for those parts to the extent applicable to compilations of such works.

Independent verification should be sought for any data, advice or recommendations contained in this book. In addition, no responsibility is assumed by the publisher for any injury and/or damage to persons or property arising from any methods, products, instructions, ideas or otherwise contained in this publication.

This publication is designed to provide accurate and authoritative information with regard to the subject matter covered herein. It is sold with the clear understanding that the Publisher is not engaged in rendering legal or any other professional services. If legal or any other expert assistance is required, the services of a competent person should be sought. FROM A DECLARATION OF PARTICIPANTS JOINTLY ADOPTED BY A COMMITTEE OF THE AMERICAN BAR ASSOCIATION AND A COMMITTEE OF PUBLISHERS.

Additional color graphics may be available in the e-book version of this book.

Library of Congress Cataloging-in-Publication Data

ISBN: 978-1-63483-263-2

Published by Nova Science Publishers, Inc. † New York

CONTENTS

PREFACE

Little public data are available to assess the extent to which sponsors of defined benefit plans are offering participants immediate lump sums to replace their lifetime annuities, but certain laws and regulations provide incentives for use of this practice. Although the U.S. Department of Labor (DOL) has primary responsibility for overseeing pension sponsors' reporting requirements, it does not require sponsors to report such lump sum offers, making oversight difficult. Pension experts generally agree that there has been a recent increase in these types of offers. Since 2012, a number of large pension plan sponsors have given selected participants a limited-time option of receiving their retirement benefits in the form of a lump sum. Although sponsors' decisions to make certain lump sum "window" offers may be permissible by law, questions have been raised about participants' understanding of the financial tradeoffs associated with their choice. This book focuses on the prevalence of lump sum offers and sponsors' incentives to use them; the implications for participants; and the extent to which selected lump sum materials provided to participants include key information.

In: Private Pensions, Lump Sum Offer… ISBN: 978-1-63483-263-2
Editor: James G. Hughes

Chapter 1

PRIVATE PENSIONS: PARTICIPANTS NEED BETTER INFORMATION WHEN OFFERED LUMP SUMS THAT REPLACE THEIR LIFETIME BENEFITS*

United States Government Accountability Office

WHY GAO DID THIS STUDY

Since 2012, a number of large pension plan sponsors have given selected participants a limited-time option of receiving their retirement benefits in the form of a lump sum. Although sponsors' decisions to make certain lump sum "window" offers may be permissible by law, questions have been raised about participants' understanding of the financial tradeoffs associated with their choice. GAO was asked to review critical issues associated with these types of offers.

This report focuses on 1) the prevalence of lump sum offers and sponsors' incentives to use them, 2) the implications for participants, and 3) the extent to which selected lump sum materials provided to participants include key information. To conduct this work, GAO identified sponsors offering lump sum windows and used social media to identify participants given offers. GAO

* This is an edited, reformatted and augmented version of a United States Government Accountability Office publication, No. GAO-15-74, dated January 2015.

reviewed 11 informational packets acquired through interviews with selected plan sponsors and participants. GAO also analyzed lump sum calculations and interviewed federal officials and pension experts.

WHAT GAO RECOMMENDS

GAO recommends that DOL improve oversight by requiring plan sponsors to notify the agency when they implement lump sum windows, and coordinate with Treasury to clarify guidance on the information sponsors provide to participants. Further, Treasury should reassess regulations governing relative value statements, as well as the interest rates and mortality tables used in calculating lump sums. Agencies generally agreed with GAO's recommendations.

WHAT GAO FOUND

Little public data are available to assess the extent to which sponsors of defined benefit plans are offering participants immediate lump sums to replace their lifetime annuities, but certain laws and regulations provide incentives for use of this practice. Although the U.S. Department of Labor (DOL) has primary responsibility for overseeing pension sponsors' reporting requirements, it does not require sponsors to report such lump sum offers, making oversight difficult. Pension experts generally agree that there has been a recent increase in these types of offers. By reviewing the limited public information that is available, GAO identified 22 plan sponsors who had offered lump sum windows in 2012, involving approximately 498,000 participants and resulting in lump sum payouts totaling more than $9.25 billion. Most of these payouts went to participants who had separated from employment and were not yet retired, but some went to retirees already receiving pension benefits. Sponsors are currently afforded enhanced financial incentives to make these offers by certain laws and regulations issued by the U.S. Department of the Treasury (specifically the Internal Revenue Service) governing the interest rates and mortality tables used to calculate lump sums.

Participants potentially face a reduction in their retirement assets when they accept a lump sum offer. The amount of the lump sum payment may be less than what it would cost in the retail market to replace the plan's benefit because the mortality and interest rates used by retail market insurers are different from the rates used by sponsors, particularly when calculating lump sums for younger participants and women. Participants who assume management of their lump sum payment gain control of their assets but also face potential investment challenges. In addition, some participants may not continue to save their lump sum payment for retirement but instead may spend some or all of it.

GAO reviewed 11 packets of informational materials provided by sponsors offering lump sums to as many as 248,000 participants and found that the packets consistently lacked key information needed to make an informed decision or were otherwise unclear. Using various sources, including financial advisors, federal agency publications, laws, and regulations, GAO identified eight key types of information that participants need to have a sound understanding of a lump sum offer. While GAO did not review the packets for compliance or legal adequacy, most packets provided a substantial amount of this key information. However, all of the packets GAO reviewed lacked at least some key information. For example, the relative value notices were often unclear about how the value of the lump sum compared to the value of the lifetime monthly benefit provided by the plan. Similarly, many packets did not clearly indicate the interest rate or mortality assumptions used, limiting participants' ability to assess how the lump sum payment was calculated. Further, few of the packets informed participants about the benefit protections they would keep by staying in their employer's plan—full or partial protections provided by the Pension Benefit Guaranty Corporation, the agency that insures defined benefit pensions when a sponsor defaults. This omission is notable because many participants GAO interviewed cited fear of sponsor default as an important factor in choosing the lump sum.

ABBREVIATIONS

CRS	Congressional Research Service
DOL	Department of Labor
EBSA	Employee Benefits Security Administration
ERISA	Employee Retirement Income Security Act of 1974
IRA	Individual Retirement Account
IRS	Internal Revenue Service
MAP-21	Moving Ahead for Progress in the 21st Century Act

PBGC	Pension Benefit Guaranty Corporation
PPA	Pension Protection Act of 2006
SEC	Securities and Exchange Commission
SOA	Society of Actuaries
TSR	Treasury Securities Rate

* * *

January 27, 2015

The Honorable Sander Levin
Ranking Member
Committee on Ways and Means
House of Representatives

Dear Mr. Levin:

Approximately 32 million U.S. workers and retirees participate in private sector single-employer defined benefit plans[1]—the type of pension plan that generally provides a lifetime monthly benefit based on a formula specified in the plan. Under this type of plan, employer-sponsors typically bear the risks associated with investing the plan's assets and ensuring that sufficient funds are available to pay the benefits to plan participants as they come due.[2] However, during 2012, a number of large private sector sponsors of defined benefit plans acted to reduce their pension liabilities by essentially transferring the liabilities to other parties. Through one particular type of risk transfer action, sponsors offered to pay some participants—including participants already retired and receiving a monthly pension—the estimated present value of their lifetime benefit in one immediate lump sum payment. This action, commonly referred to as a "lump sum window," presents certain participants with a choice of keeping their lifetime retirement annuity or taking the lump sum amount. Participants who accept the lump sum assume all the risks of managing the funds themselves. Further, their retirement benefits are no longer governed by the Employee Retirement Income Security Act of 1974 (ERISA), as amended,[3] including the guarantees provided by the Pension Benefit Guaranty Corporation (PBGC), which insures benefits from private sector defined benefit plans up to certain statutory limits. In light of these and other consequences for those accepting lump sums, you and Representative George Miller requested that GAO study what is spurring sponsors to make such offers and the potential effect these offers have on participants' retirement security.

This review addresses (1) the extent to which sponsors of defined benefit plans are transferring risk through the use of lump sum windows, and the incentives for sponsors to take such actions, (2) the implications for participants who accept a lump sum payment, and (3) the extent to which sponsors' lump sum window information materials enable participants to make an informed decision.

To identify the extent that sponsors are using lump sums windows, we collected and analyzed available information about lump sum offers implemented by plan sponsors during 2012. We obtained documents from the Securities and Exchange Commission (SEC), PBGC, the Pension Rights Center, consulting firms, and sponsors. To explore sponsors' incentives for making lump sum offers, we interviewed managers from three plan sponsors who took such actions, as well as other stakeholders, such as consultants, insurance company representatives, independent fiduciaries, and subject matter experts. To explore the implications for participants, we consulted retirement security experts and reviewed associated literature. We also used social media to identify and interview pension plan participants whose sponsor had offered them a lump sum payment. Specifically, we contacted alumni groups associated with sponsors whom we had identified as having carried out lump sum windows. We solicited input from plan participants who had been offered lump sums and administered a questionnaire to 37 participants who had contacted us. These individuals were associated with 11 plan sponsors. Of the group, we interviewed 33 to gather additional information. We also collected information materials provided to participants by all 11 of the sponsors. While not generalizable, participants' responses helped inform our discussion about the factors participants weighed when making benefit choices. In addition, we developed a lump sum calculator to generate lump sum amounts based on participant information obtained during our interviews. Using the calculator, we mimicked sponsor lump sum calculations to gain a better understanding of how certain provisions in federal law and regulations affect lump sum amounts, and we evaluated whether the rules advantage either sponsors or participants in how the amounts are calculated. Lastly, to determine the adequacy of the lump sum offer materials sponsors provide to participants, we identified key types of information participants need to make an informed decision based on a review of publications by federal agencies, financial advisors, and various other sources. We then evaluated the contents of 11 packets of information materials, each from a different sponsor's lump sum window offer, to determine whether the packets included this information. We also asked the participants we interviewed about the completeness and understandability of the information materials they had been given.

We conducted this performance audit from March 2013 to January 2015 in accordance with generally accepted government auditing standards. Those standards require that we plan and perform the audit to obtain sufficient, appropriate evidence to provide a reasonable basis for our findings and conclusions based on our audit objectives. We believe that the evidence obtained provides a reasonable basis for our findings and conclusions based on our audit objectives.

BACKGROUND

Pension De-risking and Risk Transfers

Sponsors of defined benefit pension plans are responsible for managing the financial risks associated with their plans' general administration. Such risks can include fluctuations in the value of plan assets and in interest rates, either of which can cause volatility in the plan's funded status and plan contributions.[4] This type of volatility has been exacerbated by recent fluctuations in the national economy, while a 2006 accounting standard change caused pension funding status to take a more prominent role on private sector plan sponsors' balance sheets, making such volatility more visible.[5] Over the past several decades, many sponsors have chosen to lessen their exposure to such financial risks by shifting away from defined benefit plans and choosing to offer or emphasize defined contribution plans, such as 401(k) plans, whereby the various risks are borne by the participants whose sustainable retirement income will depend on factors such as the participants' contribution decisions, the investment returns on their personal accounts, their spend-down decisions in retirement, and their longevity.[6] Likewise, sponsors who have chosen to retain their defined benefit plans have taken steps to reduce their plans' financial risks by other means. In some cases, these steps have also resulted in the transfer of risk to participants.

The steps sponsors can take to limit the financial risks they see posed by their plans are commonly referred to as pension "de-risking." Broadly speaking, de-risking actions can be divided into two groups, internal and external methods. [7] Internal methods of de-risking—although beyond the scope of our study—allow the plan sponsor to reduce risk without directly removing liabilities, or participants, from the plan. These methods may include restricting plan participation or modifying the benefit formula to reduce future benefit accruals. They may also include adjustments to the allocation of plan assets, such as by liability-driven investing. This may involve shifting away from equities and toward fixed income securities that match the duration of plan liabilities in order to shield the plan from risks associated with market fluctuations in both stock market values and interest rates. Although these internal methods allow sponsors to mitigate some of the risks associated with their plans, the existing liabilities remain in the plans and, as a result, continue to expose sponsors to certain remaining risks. For example, plan sponsors continue to be subject to the longevity risk of plan participants living longer than anticipated.

External approaches, on the other hand, involve permanently removing a portion of pension liabilities from the plan, discharging the obligation to pay a lifetime annuity to plan participants. Two of these approaches can be appropriately termed "risk transfers" because the risks of providing pension income or managing pension assets are essentially transferred to another party outside the plan. One form of risk transfer—also beyond the scope of our study—is the purchase of a "buy-out" group annuity, whereby plan assets are transferred to an insurance company that then assumes the responsibility for making pension benefit payments to participants removed from the plan. When a sponsor implements an annuity buyout, the risks associated with providing promised pension benefits are shifted from the plan sponsor to the insurer. In 2012, two large plan sponsors, General Motors and Verizon, purchased group annuities from Prudential Insurance Company involving the transfer of a reported $32.6 billion in plan liabilities.

A second form of risk transfer is a "lump sum window" offer—the form of risk transfer that is the focus of our study. Any lump sum window offer must satisfy applicable requirements under the Internal Revenue Code.[8] In a lump sum window offer, the participant is offered a choice between three optional forms of his or her benefits accrued to date. Generally, the participants who are given the offer will be separated participants—participants no longer employed by the sponsor—waiting for their pension annuity to begin in the future, or retirees already receiving their pension annuity payments.[9] The three options are as follows:

1) *Annuity at normal retirement age (or current annuity)* – In the case of a separated participant not yet in pay status, this is their lifetime annuity promised under the plan that would begin at a future date,

often age 65. In the case of a retiree in pay status, it is the lifetime annuity they are currently receiving.

2) *Immediate annuity (or alternate annuity)* – In the case of a separated participant not yet in pay status, this is their lifetime annuity promised under the plan, with payments beginning at the time of the lump sum offer rather than at their normal retirement age. The payments are reduced by a specified factor to account for the earlier commencement of benefits. In the case of a retiree in pay status, it is the lifetime annuity they are currently receiving, but they may have the option of changing to another form of benefit offered under the plan.[10]
3) *Lump sum* – In the case of both a separated participant not yet in pay status or a retiree in pay status, this is the actuarial equivalent of the remaining expected payments of their lifetime annuity, given to them in a single immediate payment.

The participant then has a limited amount of time, or window, to choose between the three options. When participants elect to receive their benefit as a lump sum, the risks involved in providing retirement income are thus transferred from the sponsor to the participants.

ERISA and Federal Oversight

ERISA establishes protections for plan participants and their beneficiaries, and sets minimum funding standards for pension plans that are sponsored by private employers, among other provisions. One broad protection offered by ERISA is the requirement that sponsors be subject to fiduciary standards in their management and administration of the plan. As fiduciaries under ERISA, sponsors are required to administer the plan solely in the interest of participants and beneficiaries and for the exclusive purpose of providing benefits and defraying plan expenses.[11] However, some functions, such as those related to establishing a plan and choosing its design features, are considered settlor functions that are not subject to ERISA's fiduciary standards. For example, a sponsor's decision to take risk transfer actions, such as offering a lump sum window, is a matter of plan design, generally making it a settlor function rather than a fiduciary function. However, once the sponsor embarks on implementation of the strategy, such action would fall within the realm of its fiduciary role, requiring the sponsor to operate in the best interest of participants and beneficiaries.

The administration of ERISA is divided among three federal agencies: the Department of Labor (DOL), the Department of the Treasury (specifically the Internal Revenue Service [IRS]), and the Pension Benefit Guaranty Corporation (PBGC). DOL takes primary responsibility for ERISA reporting and disclosure requirements. In addition, DOL promulgates regulations and produces guidance related to reporting and disclosure. Within DOL, the mission of the Employee Benefits Security Administration (EBSA) includes efforts to ensure the security of Americans' retirement benefits by assisting and educating plan participants, plan sponsors, service providers, and fiduciaries. To that end, EBSA develops regulations and enforces the law, including ERISA's fiduciary standards.[12] As GAO has reported previously, certain disclosures are specifically required to be written in a manner calculated to be understood by the average participant, and for disclosures that do not include such a requirement, DOL officials have noted that ERISA's basic fiduciary standards require that fiduciaries consider how understandable the disclosures are.[13]

ERISA also created the ERISA Advisory Council to advise the Secretary of Labor.[14] The council has carried out its role by studying testimony and deliberating on various topics and submitting recommendations regarding the Secretary's functions under ERISA. Due to the recent heightened interest in risk transfers and their perceived increase in popularity, the council held hearings in 2013 exclusively focused on such actions and the effects they may have on plan participants.[15] In its final report summarizing the hearings, the council observed that there had been an increased level of activity by sponsors to reduce or eliminate the risks associated with their pension plan liabilities and concluded with several recommendations to DOL. For example, the council recommended that disclosures associated with lump sum windows include information which enables a participant to make an informed decision. In addition, the council recommended DOL consider collecting relevant information at the time sponsors take risk transfer actions.

For its part, the IRS determines whether private sector pension plans qualify for preferential tax treatment under the Internal Revenue Code. Qualified pension plans receive favorable tax treatment, generally including the deferral of taxes on contributions and investment earnings until benefits are received. To be qualified, a plan must meet a number of requirements. Plan sponsors can request a determination letter that addresses the qualified status of the plan. In addition, a plan sponsor can request that the IRS address a unique issue requiring immediate guidance that is not likely to be provided through the determination letter process. If the IRS determines that it is in the interest of good tax administration to respond to this request, its response, known as a private letter ruling, will interpret and apply tax laws to the sponsor's represented set of facts. By law, this specific ruling may not be used or cited as precedent by other taxpayers or by IRS personnel.[16]

Also, to protect the value of each participant's pension benefit, the Internal Revenue Code prescribes the interest rate and mortality table that the sponsor must use to calculate the minimum amount of any lump sum option.[17] A plan may pay a larger lump sum, but it may not pay less than this prescribed minimum. Further, sponsors are required to provide several specific pieces of information to the participant as part of the offer.[18] For example, sponsors, when distributing pension benefits in any form, are required to provide notices to participants detailing tax implications, rollover options,[19] and a description of the financial effect of electing an optional form of benefit. As part of this description, the participant must receive a statement comparing the relative value of the new form of benefit to their original benefit. For instance, when an optional lump sum would replace a monthly annuity, participants must be shown how the lump sum compares to the value of that annuity.[20] Also, in order to receive the benefit in a form other than an annuity, such as a lump sum, the participant (and if married, the spouse) must receive and sign a waiver consenting to this alternative form of payment.[21]

The PBGC, also established by ERISA, acts as an insurer of private-sector defined benefit pension plans by guaranteeing participants' benefits up to certain statutory limits. In the case of covered single-employer plans, PBGC protects participants if the plan terminates with insufficient assets to pay all benefits, such as in the bankruptcy of a plan sponsor with an underfunded plan. Under ERISA, plan sponsors pay premiums to PBGC to help fund its guarantees. The law currently requires sponsors to pay both a per-participant flat rate premium and a variable rate premium based on the plan's level of underfunding. PBGC also collects a termination premium from sponsors who terminate their plans under certain criteria.

In both the case of a sponsor's buyout through a group annuity purchase and the case of a participant's acceptance of a lump sum payment, the participant loses the protections of ERISA and the guarantees offered by PBGC. Group annuities provided by an insurance company are guaranteed by state benefit guaranty associations up to certain levels established by the state. Lump sum payments carry no guarantees with respect to the amount and duration of future retirement income they may ultimately provide.

Little Is Known about the Extent of Lump Sum Windows, though Cost-Saving Incentives May Be Encouraging Sponsor Use

Data are lacking about the prevalence of lump sum windows, as there are no requirements that sponsors report when they use this practice. However, experts in the field of retirement pensions, including DOL's ERISA Advisory Council, generally maintain that since 2012 an increasing number of sponsors have used lump sum window offers to shed plan liabilities. The offers we identified included offers made to separated vested participants not yet receiving benefits, as well as offers targeted to retirees who were already receiving benefit payments. While lump sum windows have the effect of reducing the size of sponsors' pension plans, thereby reducing sponsors' financial risk, the recent reported increase in use may reflect enhanced financial cost-saving incentives for such actions. These include changing federal laws and regulations governing the interest rates and mortality tables used to calculate lump sums, and those affecting PBGC premium rates. Likewise, other longstanding rules may also serve as incentives to act. Sponsors must also take into account their unique business circumstances and certain disincentives associated with lump sum windows.

Full Extent of Lump Sum Offers Is Unknown

Comprehensive data on the details and the number of lump sum window offers are not publicly available. Although DOL takes primary responsibility for ERISA reporting requirements, neither it nor the other two agencies that oversee ERISA provisions, IRS and PBGC, are required to track or compile comprehensive data on such offers. As a result, the information currently required to be reported by sponsors when they implement lump sum windows is insufficient to provide a complete picture of the extent of the practice.[22] For example, whenever lump sums are paid out from a pension fund, the sponsor is required to report the payout to IRS.[23] However, such reporting does not distinguish payouts associated with a lump sum window from other types of payouts from pension funds, such as monthly annuity payments. In addition, some sponsors may choose to disclose limited information about lump sum window offers within their annual corporate reports and some may do so as part of periodic filings to the SEC. However, absent more specific requirements to report on lump sum window offers, meaningful data on the extent of their use do not exist.

Nevertheless, pension experts generally agree that sponsors' use of lump sum windows has become more frequent in recent years. In summarizing its 2013 hearings on pension de-risking, the ERISA Advisory Council concluded that the testimony they had heard served to confirm that risk transfer actions, such as lump sum windows, are on the rise. Studies cited by leading pension consulting firms, albeit without full disclosure of their data and study methods, have furthered this perception. Citing proprietary data, one firm has estimated that nearly 200 sponsors implemented lump sum windows during 2012.[24] That firm reported that its survey of 180 plan sponsors found that 26 percent had implemented a lump sum window in 2012, and another 41 percent were in the process of, or considering, taking such action between 2013 and 2015.[25] Another firm reported that its study indicated that of 223 sponsors surveyed, 12 percent had recently implemented a lump sum window. Of the remaining sponsors, 43 percent were reported to have said they were very or somewhat likely to do so in 2014.[26]

Through our own search of publicly available data, we were able to identify 22 plan sponsors who had offered lump sum windows to their plan participants in 2012.[27] While this likely represents only a portion of the actual number of sponsors offering lump sum windows during this time, these 22 cases alone involved offers to approximately 498,000 participants.[28] Public data on the dollar amount of lump sums paid were limited, but for the 16 sponsors providing this information, we found the total payouts to be just over $9.25 billion in 2012. Based on its study of lump sum windows completed during 2012, a pension consulting firm reported acceptance rates ranging between 25 and 85 percent, with a majority being between 45 and 65 percent.[29] Most (19 of 22) of the lump sum windows we identified only targeted participants who were not yet receiving their retirement annuity. However, three of the actions involved lump sums being offered to retired participants who had already begun receiving annuity payments.

According to many pension experts, the lump sum windows implemented by Ford Motor Company and General Motors Company in 2012 could be viewed as a new approach to the practice, as they were reported to be the first known instances of lump sum offers to retirees in payment status rather than to separated vested participants not yet retired. Prior to implementation, it was also widely reported that both sponsors had requested and obtained IRS private letter rulings stating that their actions would "not fail to satisfy" certain provisions of the Internal Revenue Code. [30] According to the letters, one important question was whether such lump sums would violate existing rules governing the amount and benefit payment period.[31] In both private letter rulings, IRS concluded that such actions were permissible because the lump sum option was being offered pursuant to a plan amendment and only during a limited window period.[32]

Cost Savings Provide Incentive for Sponsors to Offer Lump Sum Windows

Substantial financial advantages exist for plan sponsors considering implementing lump sum windows. In general, sponsors' use of lump sum windows reduces the size of their pension plans, which can result in reduced financial volatility for the sponsor's cash flow, income statement, and balance sheet, as well as reduced administrative burden and costs. However, changing federal laws and regulations concerning interest rates, mortality tables, and PBGC premiums may be providing additional cost-saving incentives for more plan sponsors to offer lump sums to their plans' participants in recent years. Moreover, certain longstanding rules can also afford savings to sponsors by allowing them to offer lower lump sums by choosing an advantageous interest rate and excluding certain additional plan benefits, such as early retirement subsidies, when calculating lump sums. Lump sum windows also offer sponsors an opportunity to reduce oversized plan liabilities, such as in cases where the pension plan is large relative to the size of the plan sponsor's business. They also offer sponsors an opportunity to target specific groups of individuals, such as vested terminated participants who may have had no prior relationship to the plan sponsor because they were in a plan that had been taken over as part of a merger or acquisition deal. At the same time, implementation of lump sum windows also involves costs. Sponsors have to weigh both the incentives and disincentives before taking such actions in order to determine if implementing a lump sum window addresses their unique business goals in a cost-effective manner.

Recent and Impending Rule Changes That Provide Incentives for Lump Sum Windows

The federal laws and regulations regarding how lump sums are calculated have been changing in recent years. From the sponsor's perspective, these changes make it more advantageous to implement a lump sum window at this time. Rules concerning interest rates have become more favorable, making it more advantageous to implement a lump sum window now and in the future than it was in the past. Impending changes to mortality tables provide an incentive to implement a lump sum window now to realize a potential financial cost-savings, an opportunity that will likely disappear when new mortality tables are adopted. Rising PBGC premiums also provide an ongoing and rising incentive for some plan sponsors to remove liabilities from the plan via a lump sum window or some other means.

Switch to More Favorable Interest Rates

Recent changes to the rules regarding how lump sums are calculated allow the use of interest rates that can result in lower lump sums for participants, which would be advantageous to plan sponsors trying to minimize the cost of implementing a lump sum window offer.

Illustration of How PPA Rules on Interest Rates Can Affect Lump Sums

Bob is 45, has a lifetime deferred retirement pension of $10,000 a year starting at age 65, and was offered a lump sum in October 2012.

Prior to PPA, Bob's immediate lump sum would have been $62,643, calculated based on a 30-year Treasury interest rate of 3.65 percent.[a]

After PPA, Bob's immediate lump sum is $32,453, calculated based on a corporate bond interest rate of 6.02 percent, or 48 percent less than it would have been under rules prior to PPA.[b]

Source: GAO analysis. | GAO-15-74

[a]For this comparison, Treasury and corporate bond interest rates as of August 2011 were used for the October 2012 calculation, as permitted under current law. For more details on our analysis of how the change to interest rates under PPA affects lump sum amounts, see appendix II.

[b]Under PPA, different interest rates are used to discount future benefits based on the number of years in the future the benefits will be paid. For a 45-year-old individual, with benefits assumed to be paid 20 or more years in the future, a single interest rate of 6.02 percent is used for this October 2012 calculation. Note that the negative impact of the PPA rule change on lump sum amounts will typically be greater for younger participants than older participants.

Prior to enactment of the Pension Protection Act of 2006 (PPA), sponsors were required to calculate lump sums using interest rates on 30-year Treasury bonds. Since PPA, sponsors have been allowed to use generally higher corporate bond interest rates,[33] which can serve to lower the amount of the lump sums offered to many participants.34,35 A consulting firm estimated that, because of the general reduction in lump sum amounts resulting from this rule change, one of their client sponsors paying out $40 million in lump sums could potentially save about $10 million due to the switch to the higher rates. The PPA switch from Treasury bond rates to corporate bond rates became fully effective in 2012, and some experts believe that this timing may partly explain the reported recent increase in risk transfers since 2012.[36]

In addition, the Moving Ahead for Progress in the 21st Century Act (MAP-21) allowed more sponsors to take advantage of this rule change by temporarily raising the interest rates that can be used to value plan liabilities,[37] significantly improving many plans' reported funded status, which in turn allowed more plan sponsors to consider offering lump-sum payouts.[38]

Current Mortality Tables

The mortality tables which sponsors must use in determining minimum lump sum amounts provide another incentive to conduct a lump sum window at this time. This is because the tables currently required for this purpose under IRS regulations do not reflect the accelerated rate of longevity improvements that have occurred in recent years. These longevity improvements have been reflected in updated mortality tables recently released by the Society of Actuaries (SOA) and they are expected to be adopted by IRS for lump sum calculations, but possibly not until 2016.[39] The new SOA tables reflect a longer life expectancy for individuals, and when used to calculate lump sums will yield correspondingly larger lump sum amounts.[40] Thus, sponsors making lump sum offers prior to IRS's anticipated adoption of the new tables can realize substantial financial savings since their lump sum calculations will still be based on older tables. According to SOA, the new mortality tables reflect a 10.4 to 11.3 percent longer life expectancy for individuals age 65 in 2014[41]—increases that could translate into lump sums that are markedly greater than those based on the current tables used for 2014 lump sum calculations.[42] Therefore, sponsors with lump sum payouts exceeding, for example, $100 million could potentially save millions of dollars by taking action before the adoption of new mortality tables, all other factors remaining the same.

Prior to SOA's release of the new tables, in August 2013, IRS announced that the currently required tables will continue to be used for the calculation of minimum lump sum payments in 2014 and 2015, and IRS officials we interviewed said there is currently no timetable for when it will adopt new tables. They said nothing precludes IRS from adopting new tables prior to 2016, but they said it will not occur until the agency completes its issuance process. Several pension experts are of the opinion that the switch is not likely to occur until at least 2016. Until then, sponsors can continue to use the current mortality tables and generate relatively lower lump sums, providing a window of opportunity to implement a lump sum window at lower cost than in the future.

Illustration of How Use of Current versus New Mortality Tables Can Affect Lump Sums

Jane is 45, has a lifetime deferred retirement pension of $10,000 a year starting at age 65, and was offered a lump sum in October 2012.

Jane's immediate lump sum would be $35,944, calculated based on new mortality tables reflecting more up-to-date longevity estimates.

Jane's immediate lump sum is $32,453, calculated based on current mortality tables, or 10 percent less than it would be using the new tables.[a]

Source: GAO analysis. | GAO-15-74

[a]For the relative impact of using current mortality tables across several ages, see appendix II.

Rising PBGC Premiums

Recent federal legislation that has increased PBGC premium rates, as well as scheduled additional future increases, creates another potential cost-saving incentive for sponsors to conduct a lump sum window offer.[43] PBGC premiums are based, in part, on the number of participants in a plan, so reducing the number of participants via a lump sum window directly reduces the total amount of the annual premium for that sponsor. The flat rate portion of the single-employer premium rose 63 percent— from $35 to $57 per participant—between 2012 and 2015. Further, this rate is scheduled to increase another 12 percent, to $64 per participant, in 2016, for an overall rate increase of 83 percent from 2012 to 2016.[44] Thus, for each participant that had been removed from a plan prior to 2015, the sponsor reduced its 2015 PBGC single-employer, flat rate premium costs by $57. Likewise, removal of participants in 2016 will result in similar savings.[45]

Terminated vested participants can be a particularly attractive group through which to achieve PBGC premium savings through a lump sum offer since they often represent a large portion of a population but a small portion of the participant liabilities.[46] According to a leading consultant's analysis of selected plans, terminated vested participants can represent less than one-sixth of the total amount of liabilities in single-employer pension plans but nearly a third of the total plan participant counts.[47] As a result, terminated vested participants can account for a significant portion of a plan's ongoing administrative expense, such as PBGC premiums. A sponsor can generate significant administrative cost savings, especially for large plans, if they can remove participants and their associated premium costs from the plan. Experts differ in their opinion of the extent to which rising PBGC premium rates act as an incentive for sponsors to implement a lump sum window. Notably, two of the sponsors we spoke to said the rate increases did not factor into their decision to any great extent. However, one said they were a concern and that the impending premium increases could prompt them to take further action in the future.

Longstanding Rules That Provide Incentives for Lump Sum Windows

In addition to recent and impending changes in federal rules, certain longstanding federal rules can also act as financial incentives to sponsors considering implementing a lump sum window by potentially reducing the size of lump sum amounts or by allowing the sponsor to avoid potential plan costs.

Ability to Choose a "Lookback" Rate

One longstanding IRS rule that can sometimes provide a significant financial incentive for offering a lump sum window is the provision that permits plan sponsors to select the interest rate used for lump sum calculations from up to 17 months prior to the month of the lump sum offer. This interest rate is commonly known as a "lookback" rate.[48] IRS officials we interviewed pointed out that when used for the calculation of lump sums that are part of a plan's ongoing design (not a lump sum window situation), this rule can work to the advantage of either the plan sponsor or the plan participant at different points in time, depending on whether interest rates have decreased or increased since the "lookback" month. However, when used in association with a one-time lump sum window with a fixed payment date, the "lookback" rate can be selectively used to financial advantage by plan sponsors when interest rates have decreased.[49] This is because it allows sponsors to choose favorable interest rates that are higher than prevailing rates, resulting in smaller lump sum payouts.[50] In 2012, as interest rates were declining, this rule allowed plans to look back to higher rates from as early as August 2011. Of the 11 sponsors whose information packets we examined, all sponsors who disclosed the interest rates used for the lump sum calculations had used sponsor-favorable "lookback" interest rates from between 11 and 16 months prior to the lump sum payment date.

Illustration of How the "Lookback" Rules on Interest Rates Can Affect Lump Sums

Dan is 45, has a lifetime deferred retirement pension of $10,000 a year starting at age 65, and was offered a lump sum in October 2012.

Dan's immediate lump sum would have been $46,967, calculated based on prevailing interest rates as of September 2012, the month prior to the lump sum offer.

Dan's immediate lump sum is $32,453, calculated based on "lookback" rates as of August 2011, or 31 percent less than it would have been using a rate as of the month prior to the offer.[a]

Source: GAO analysis. | GAO-15-74

[a]Note that the negative impact of the "lookback" rule on lump sum amounts will often be greater for younger participants than older participants. For the relative impact of the "lookback" rule across several ages, see appendix II.

Ability to Exclude Certain Additional Plan Benefits

Another longstanding rule that provides an incentive for offering a lump sum window is the rule that allows sponsors to exclude certain additional plan benefits when calculating the amount of the lump sum. These additional plan benefits that are sometimes provided by pension plans include subsidized early retirement benefits, subsidized joint-and-survivor benefits, and supplemental early retirement benefits.[51] Although a separated participant, in the absence of a lump sum window, might have gone on to be eligible for and collect such additional benefits in the future, or might already be eligible for such benefits, the lump sum may still be calculated assuming the participant would have collected a normal retirement benefit without any additional benefits.[52]

Illustration of How the Exclusion of Early Retirement Subsidies Can Affect Lump Sums

Pam is 45, has a lifetime deferred retirement pension of $10,000 a year starting at age 65, but also qualifies for a subsidized, unreduced early retirement benefit starting at age 60. She was offered a lump sum in October 2012.

Pam's immediate lump sum would have been $54,301, if the lump sum is calculated assuming that Pam would have retired at age 60, i.e., if the early retirement subsidy had been included in the lump sum calculation.

Pam's immediate lump sum is $32,453, if the lump sum is calculated assuming that Pam would have retired at age 65, i.e., if the early retirement subsidy was not included in the lump sum calculation, or 40 percent less than it would have been if the subsidized, unreduced early retirement benefit was included.

Source: GAO analysis.

Other Considerations

In addition to these potential incentives, sponsors and experts say the decision to implement a lump sum window is often driven by how large the sponsor's pension liabilities have become in comparison to the overall size of the business. This consideration takes on particular importance when a business downsizes or, conversely, acquires other companies. Indeed, two of the three sponsors we spoke to said recent restructuring of their companies had resulted in their plan's liabilities becoming unacceptably large relative to the overall size of the business. Both had recently experienced significant downsizing of their core business, yet both had retained large amounts of benefit obligations owed to participants. This particular issue was also mentioned by one of the sponsors who requested an IRS private letter ruling prior to offering lump sums to retirees in pay status. The sponsor had stated that the pension obligations reported on the company's financial statements had become "disproportionately large" and very sensitive to swings in interest rates. They explained that such volatility increases the cost of financing, makes cash flow management more difficult, and makes the company less competitive in the marketplace.[53] The sponsors we talked to said their decision to reduce their pension liabilities was a means to shore up their overall balance sheet.

The other sponsor we interviewed told us that, in their case, their business had grown due to the acquisition of other companies. However, with the mergers had come additional pension liabilities and costs associated with the defined benefit plans of the acquired companies. They said they were now burdened with pension costs associated with separated vested participants who had never been directly associated with their corporation. This sponsor told us they implemented a lump sum window primarily on the advice of their pension consultant, who presented the action as a cost-effective means of reducing administrative burden and costs associated these types of separated participants.[54]

Disincentives to Offering a Lump Sum Window

Implementing a lump sum window is not cost-free for plan sponsors. Despite the potential incentives, many experts point out that the decision to implement a lump sum window will be based on each sponsor's unique business considerations, and potential downsides must be considered. Disincentives include the administrative costs involved, future costs associated with adverse selection, the need to make sizeable immediate payments, interest rate uncertainty, and foregone potential returns.[55]

- **Administrative costs.** Conducting a lump sum window requires sponsors to collect and verify data on their participant population to properly value their benefit obligations, which in some cases may involve the reconciliation of thousands of participant data records. In addition, participant communications, including information materials, must be prepared, and call centers may need to be set up, requiring staffing and training. If these administrative tasks are performed in-house, it will take time and resources; if outsourced to a third party, the sponsor will likely incur service fees.
- **Adverse selection.** When lump sums are offered, it is possible that relatively unhealthy participants will be more likely to accept the lump sum and, conversely, healthier participants will choose to keep their existing deferred annuity. If so, the remaining plan participants may outlive the mortality assumptions used to value liabilities, requiring additional plan funding in the future to cover benefit payments.
- **Sizeable immediate payments.** The payment of lump sums results in an immediate depletion of plan assets. In such cases, it is possible that the sponsor might have to sell assets at a poor time, when their position in the market is low. In addition, lump sum payouts could reduce the funded ratio of an underfunded plan, potentially increasing minimum required contributions.
- **Interest rate uncertainty.** Future interest rate increases can reduce the lump sum amounts to be paid, so that the sponsor might have achieved greater benefits if action had been postponed. However, the potential effect of interest rate increases on the value of plan assets would also be a consideration. For example, if a sponsor anticipates

that interest rates will rise in the future, they will need to determine whether the cost savings associated with paying lower lump sum amounts then is offset by the potential for investment losses on plan assets before the lump sum window is executed.

- **Foregone potential returns.** Lump sum payments can come at the expense of future market earnings, if future rates of return on the assets would have exceeded the interest rate used to calculate the lump sums. Foregone potential returns is a flipside of risk reduction, as reduced risk often means reduced potential rewards as well.

LUMP SUM PAYMENTS CAN LOSE VALUE FOR PARTICIPANTS IN VARIOUS WAYS

When participants of defined benefit pension plans accept lump sums, they are waiving their right to receive a lifetime income stream from their pension plan and must manage the payment received on their own from that point forward. Some may try to replicate an income stream by using their lump sum to purchase an annuity on the retail market. Others may roll over their lump sum into an Individual Retirement Account (IRA) and then invest and withdraw funds at their discretion. Still others may choose to use the lump sum to pay off debt or purchase consumer goods. While the participant may manage or spend their lump sum in ways that are beneficial to their circumstances, participants in all three of these situations are at risk of losing value from their retirement savings in various ways.

Annuitizing a Lump Sum Payment May Not Fully Replace the Value of the Plan's Annuity

In cases where participants accept the lump sum and then wish to replicate a lifetime income stream by purchasing an annuity on their own, the amount of their monthly benefit could be significantly lower than what would have been provided by their plans. It might seem counterintuitive for an individual to use a lump sum to purchase a lifetime annuity, since the individual could have just kept the lifetime annuity he or she already had from the defined benefit plan. Most of the participants we interviewed who accepted lump sum payments told us that they did not trust the security of their plan benefit (discussed further in the next section), and some said they were encouraged by others to purchase a retail annuity.

Differences between Retail and Plan Annuities

Using the lump sum to purchase a retail annuity could result in significantly less annuity income than what would have been provided by the plan because different factors are at play for sponsors converting pension annuities to lump sums than for insurance companies selling lifetime annuities on the retail market.[56] Insurers in the retail market use different interest rate assumptions and mortality tables than those used by plan sponsors to calculate minimum required lump sums, and also include other factors such as profit margins in their pricing. Additionally, unlike plan sponsors, insurers can price annuities differently for men and women when selling annuities outside the qualified retirement plan environment.

We estimated potential reductions in monthly retirement income if a participant were to accept a lump sum window offer and then use the lump sum to purchase a retail annuity. [57] In the absence of sufficient data on retail annuity prices, we based annuity purchase rates on estimated group annuity rates published by PBGC. Retail annuities for individuals are typically more expensive than group annuities. Figure 1 illustrates the potential reduction in monthly retirement income.[58] Income is reduced at all ages shown in the figure. The reduction is up to 68 percent for the youngest female (age 35), although a 35-year-old may be less likely to purchase a replacement income annuity. At ages at which people are more typically at or approaching retirement, the reductions are 24 percent and 17 percent for 65-year-old females and males, respectively, and 41 and 36 percent for 55-year-old females and males, respectively. Differences between the prices of market-based annuities and the valuation of a plan lump sum payment can be pronounced for reasons such as 1) discount rate (interest rate) differences and mortality assumption differences, 2) gender differences, and 3) differences between group and retail annuity pricing.

Differences in Actuarial Factors

As illustrated in figure 1, on average, lump sum values were insufficient to meet the group annuity purchase rates in order to replace the coverage in the retail market. This is likely due in large part to differences in the actuarial factors used to value minimum lump sums, as set by law and regulation, versus those used by insurance companies to price annuities. One such factor is the discount rates, or interest rates used to convert future projected annuity payments into a lump sum amount or an annuity price.[59] The generally higher lump sum discount rates have the effect of making the lump sum less than the amount needed to purchase a corresponding annuity, with the gap increasing at younger ages.[60] A second factor is the mortality (or longevity) assumption. As noted earlier, the mortality assumption for determining minimum lump sums has not kept up with increases in longevity and, all else equal, has the effect of making lump sums today lower than they would be with up-to-date tables. In contrast, insurance companies will factor this increased longevity into their pricing, so that this factor will also tend to make minimum lump sums insufficient to purchase a corresponding annuity.

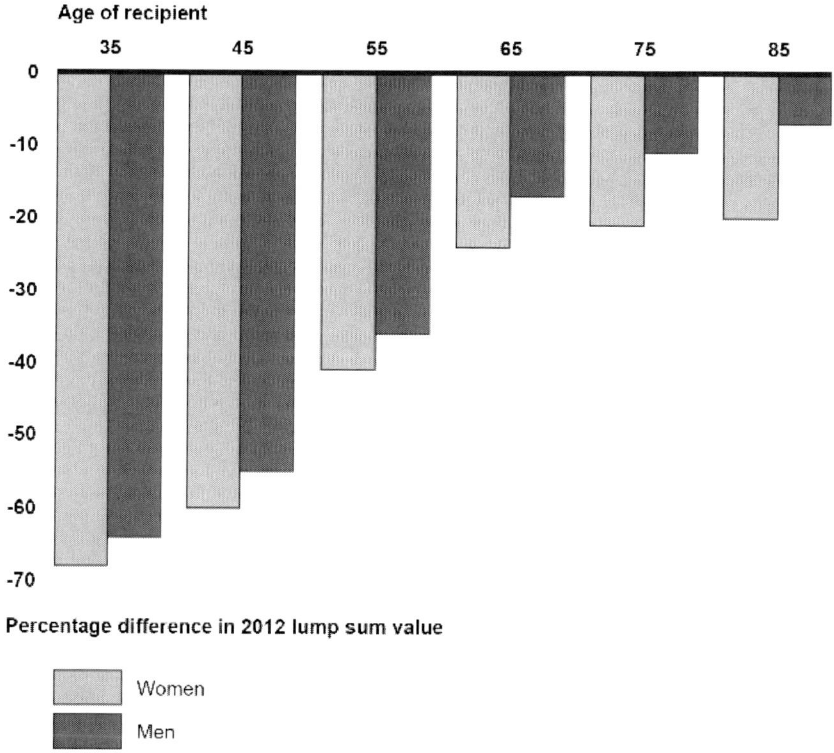

Source: GAO analysis of U.S. Department of the Treasury (Internal Revenue Service) and Pension Benefit Guaranty Corporation (PBGC) data. I GAO-15-74

Note: This figure illustrates the potential percentage reduction in monthly retirement income that a plan participant might experience by accepting a lump sum window offer and then using the lump sum to purchase an annuity outside the plan. Lump sum payment amounts were based on the minimum required methodology using assumptions that we found prevalent in participant materials.

In the absence of sufficient data on retail annuity prices, we based annuity purchase rates on estimated group annuity rates published by PBGC. Retail annuities are typically more expensive than group annuities, which would make the reductions in monthly retirement income even bigger than those illustrated here. Annuity payments are assumed to commence at age 65 for those younger than age 65. See appendix II for a more detailed discussion of this methodology.

Figure 1. Potential Percentage Reduction to Monthly Benefit with Lump Sum Purchase of Out-of-Plan Annuity.

Differences Based on Gender

The reduction in retirement income, or the gap between the amount of the lump sum offered and the amount needed, varies significantly by both the age and gender of the participant. Regarding gender differences, for example, figure 1 shows a 36 percent reduction in income for a 55 year-old male, compared to a 41 percent reduction for a 55-year-old female, from accepting a lump sum and purchasing an annuity. This gender differential occurs because federal law requires a sponsor calculating the amount of the lump sum payment to assume both men and women have the same life expectancy,[61] while an insurer offering retail annuities outside the qualified retirement plan environment generally can charge different rates to men and women. On average, women live longer than men and thus collect benefits over a longer period of time. The insurer will thus require a woman to pay more than a man of the same age to purchase an equivalent lifetime monthly benefit.

Differences in Pricing

Most participants accepting the lump sum payment, but then wishing to still have an annuity, will be subject to purchasing a more costly individual retail annuity rather than a group annuity.[62] One reason for this cost difference is that the individual retail annuity market is also subject to adverse selection, which means that when given a choice, relatively healthier individuals will tend to purchase or select annuities, increasing average costs because such individuals are expected to live longer. According to the American Academy of Actuaries, adverse selection can add about a 10 percent increase to the annuity price. Retail annuities can also include additional distribution, administrative and sales charges that can add further to their cost differential over group annuities. Moreover, certain individuals, particularly older retirees, may find that regardless of cost, they do not have the ability to purchase a lifetime annuity on their own. For example, one retail annuity site we examined would not offer lifetime annuities to individuals older than age 85. An expert also told us that some insurers will not sell a retail annuity for less than a certain price.

Certain Participants Contacted about Purchasing Annuities

Although in many instances the acceptance of a lump sum payment with the intention of purchasing a retail annuity essentially results in the exchange of a cheaper plan annuity to purchase a more expensive retail annuity, some participants have received contacts encouraging them to do so. One financial planner we spoke with told us that he noticed that a few participants who had been offered lump sums were approached by financial service providers trying to sell retail annuity products. Additionally, our interviews of participants found that a few (3) participants had received unsolicited contacts about purchasing an annuity with the lump sum. However, none of the participants that accepted a lump sum actually purchased an annuity with most of their lump sum payment. The financial planner, who advised participants affiliated with two prominent lump sum window offers in 2012, said he counseled many of the participants considering the purchase of a retail annuity to simply stay in their plan and receive lifetime annuity income through the plan.[63]

Rolling Over a Lump Sum into an IRA Brings Added Control, but also Management Risks and Challenges

Participants who elect lump sum payments and roll them over into IRAs now have the ability to control and manage their own funds. But they must also manage the risks and challenges associated with decisions regarding the investment and withdrawal of the funds that were previously the responsibility of their DB plan sponsor.[64] They may find it difficult to earn a rate of return that allows them to accumulate and withdraw the monies in amounts that replicate the benefit they gave up under the plan, or to provide protection over their entire retirement period should they live to an old age. As with any investment strategy, the participant will face a tradeoff between maximizing return with riskier investments, such as stocks, versus maintaining their assets with lower return, lower volatility investments, such as bonds.

Risks and Challenges of Asset Management

Participants who roll over their lump sums into IRAs will face risks in managing and investing the monies for later drawdown. Specifically, by making this choice, participants must contend with 1) the potential of outliving their assets; 2) complex decisions concerning the investment of the lump sum and the drawdown of the assets; and 3) the difficulty of finding trusted advice.

Outliving Assets

A major risk that participants face overall is that they may outlive their lump sum assets. Figure 2 shows how long a hypothetical lump sum, based on a $10,000 annual ($833 monthly) benefit, would last for a 45- year-old participant if the participant invested the lump sum and drew down the monies beginning at age 65. The illustration shows that the age at which the drawdown exhausts the monies is highly sensitive to the rate of return. For example, at an annualized 2 percent rate of return, the participant's monies will exhaust after 5 years at age 70. However, at an annualized 7 percent rate of return, the participant's monies will last an additional 30 years, exhausting after 35 years at age 100. While these drawdown scenarios are not specific to a participant's gender, they do highlight that women may be particularly vulnerable to outliving their assets as women tend to have longer life expectancies than men.

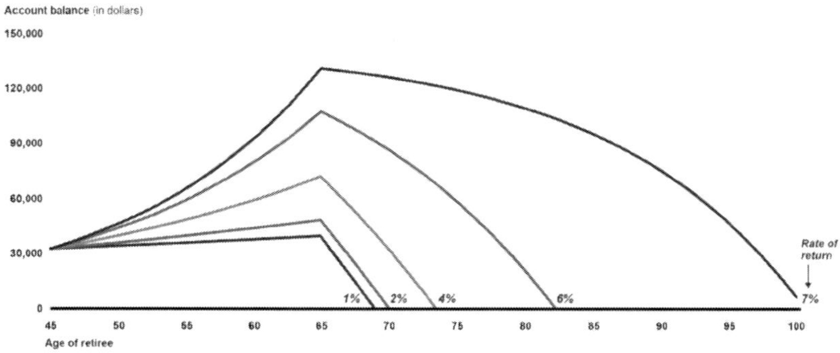

Source: GAO analysis. | GAO-15-74

Note: Hypothetical example of a 45-year-old participant who has accrued a future pension benefit of $10,000 per year ($833 monthly) starting at age 65, but who gives up the guaranteed lifetime pension benefit in exchange for a lump sum of $32,453. (Lump sum amount based on August 2011 § 417(e)(3) interest rates, and § 417(e)(3) mortality, for the 2012 plan year.) The hypothetical participant then rolls the lump sum into an interest-bearing account until retirement, and spends down the account, beginning at age 65, by the original pension amount of $833 per month.

Figure 2. Potential Age When Benefits Would Stop with Lump Sum Spend-down Matching Plan's Monthly Benefit, by Various Rates of Return.

Managing Assets Prior to and through Retirement

Participants face challenges in managing the many complex decisions involving their lump sum during both the accumulation phase prior to retirement and the spend-down phase after they begin drawing down their lump sum. These decisions are further complicated by the ups and downs of financial markets, including fluctuating rates of return, effect of fees, and deciding when and how much to withdraw, especially when spouses or other beneficiaries need to be taken into consideration.

- **Fluctuating rates of return.** Unlike the constant rates of return reflected in the preceding spend-down scenario (see figure 2), participants' investments may fluctuate, and the sequence of fluctuating rates of return can pose additional risks. For example, due to net cash outflows from a retiree's spend-down of his or her lump sum, the lump sum account has a diminishing asset base that can be particularly at risk if the retiree encounters periods of low returns or losses, as the account will have less time to recover from such downturns. Further, the continued draw-down of the account during such periods means that assets might have to be sold at depressed values, and less money will remain in the account to benefit from any future market upturn.[65]
- **Effect of fees.** As prior GAO work on fees has shown, fees can significantly decrease retirement assets. Even a small fee deducted from one's assets annually could represent a large amount of money years later had these funds remained in the account to be reinvested. This means that participants will have to carefully consider fees as they review alternative investment options. Compared to participant controlled investment in account-based pension plans, this can be more difficult in the retail market.[66]
- **Loss of budgeting signal.** A monthly pension has the advantage of providing a retiree a budgeting signal as to how much can reasonably and safely be spent each month. During the spend-down phase, this valuable information is lost when a participant converts a monthly pension into a single lump sum. The retiree may spend more of the

lump sum each month than is sustainable. In addition, the retiree may have to make large unforeseen expenditures at certain times without realizing the likely negative impact on the exhaustion date of the lump sum, whereas for a retiree receiving a monthly pension, a large expenditure can be seen relative to the monthly pension amount and may lead the retiree to take other remedial measures.[67,68] Additionally, in some cases the retiree may unnecessarily restrict his or her standard of living by spending less each month than a steady pension would have permitted.

- **Diminished capacity.** Managing assets through retirement may be particularly challenging for retirees who experience diminished physical or mental capacity as they age. For example, a retiree with dementia may find it more difficult to manage the many decisions involved with investing and drawing down an IRA compared to the relative simplicity of receiving a monthly pension check. As one scholar has noted, if the retiree misuses a monthly pension check, another check will arrive the following month. However, if the retiree makes investments that result in significant losses for their IRA, there may bc no additional funds for future withdrawal.[69]
- **Planning for spouses.** Our previous illustration assumes the money is drawn down for an individual's lifetime. Acceptance of a lump sum over $5,000 for married or formerly married individuals requires spousal consent to waive the right to a future annuity based on the combined lifetime of participant and spouse, known as a joint and survivor annuity. However, this does not preclude the participant from including a spouse or beneficiary in his retirement planning. If the participant wishes to account for his spouse's lifetime as well, he may need to add more years of spend-down, either by lowering the amount paid out per month or taking on additional investment risk in an attempt to achieve greater returns.

Finding Trusted Professional Advice

Participants assuming responsibility for managing their funds may find dealing with all these challenges difficult and may seek out professional advice to assist them. According to a DOL official, many participants are unlikely to understand the full complexity of accepting a lump sum and may not be well-equipped to manage the lump sum assets on their own. Ideally, a financial planner should be able to help people navigate the myriad decisions required to accept and manage a lump sum payment. However, participants could face additional challenges finding trusted advice in managing their assets if they do not feel comfortable managing investment and drawdown decisions on their own. Others might find it challenging to afford a financial planner. In previous work, we have found that participants can receive conflicted advice because the financial interests of those giving advice may not be aligned with the best interests of the participant.[70]

Those offering investment advice to participants may be motivated by financial gain through sales of preferred financial products, commissions, or other fees for services.[71] A few (4) individuals we interviewed noted that their advisor might have benefited more financially had they elected the lump sum, noting that the advisor was interested in managing a large sum of money.

Participant Quote

"After I received the lump sum offer there were sharks everywhere trying to convince me to let them manage the money. They really came out of the woodwork." – 60-69 year old woman.

Source: GAO's interviews with participants. | GAO-15-74.

Results of our participant questionnaire reveal that participants given lump sum offers often received unsolicited financial advice, for example, from financial planners, investment advisors, or even other plan participants. About a quarter (10 of 37) of the participants who completed our questionnaire reported being contacted by individuals not formally connected with the pension plan who offered unsolicited services directly related to the lump sum payment. For example, participants reported being contacted by individuals offering to provide tax advice, help create a retirement or financial plan, or invest the funds. Some (9) participants noted unsolicited mail and email invitations they received at the time of the lump sum offer, and being contacted by individuals offering to help them manage the money.[72]

Reasons Participants May Choose Rollover IRAs

According to prior GAO work, sponsors' service providers often may direct participants leaving employment to move their retirement savings to IRAs without any detailed knowledge of the participant's financial situation.[73] Participants may interpret information about their service providers' retail investment products as a suggestion to choose such products, which may or may not suit their ultimate retirement goals. Available evidence suggests that many participants who take lump sums choose to roll their funds into an IRA. No official statistics with respect to the disposition of lump sum window payments exist, but one retirement consultant's survey suggests that just over half of participants roll over the full amount of their lump sum into an IRA.[74] For example, the survey found that among 30 sponsor-clients representing 150,000 participants who were offered lump sum window elections in 2012, 51 percent of the participants who accepted lump sums directly rolled over their distribution into a 401(k) or an IRA.[75]

Using Lump Sums for Immediate Expenditures May Have Benefits but also Consequences for Retirement

One of the most critical decisions that participants must make with their lump sums is whether they will continue to manage their lump sum payments as part of their retirement planning goals. When participants choose to use the lump sums to pay off debts or spend the money on consumer goods, rather than keep the funds in the tax-qualified retirement system, this is often referred to as "leakage."[76] However, this "leakage" may be appropriate for some participants. They may have other uses for their payment that are beneficial to their circumstances, for example, paying health care expenses, paying for additional education that may lead to more secure employment, or bequeathing the money.

Besides potentially diminishing their retirement savings, participants who do not directly roll over all of their lump sum payment into a tax-preferred account may be subject to certain additional taxes or withholding. For example, when a participant cashes out their lump sum payment, there is an additional tax of 10 percent, in addition to ordinary income tax, if the participant is younger than age 591/2. In addition, the sponsor must withhold 20 percent of the value of the lump sum to cover federal and, if applicable, state taxes. The ultimate tax liability will depend on the participant's individual circumstances, but he or she is likely to witness some erosion in the value of the initial lump sum.

Participant Quote

"I needed the money now. I have three boys that are leaving home and [I] have medical conditions that made me think I may not live long enough to break even with the annuity." – 50-59 year old man who accepted lump sum and used part of it to pay down mortgage and medical expenses

Source: GAO's interviews with participants. | GAO-15-74

Studies have found that younger workers, lower earners, and persons with smaller distributions are most likely to take lump sums and not keep them as retirement savings.[77] On the other hand, individuals may have important immediate spending needs that must be addressed prior to retirement. Our interviews of participants presented with lump sum window offers found that only 2 of the 15 participants who accepted the lump sum cashed it out to pay for immediate expenditures. In both cases, the participants had important immediate needs associated with their expenditures. In one case the former participant used most of the lump sum to pay for living expenses; in the other the former participant used most of the monies to pay down mortgage debt.[78]

Lump Sum Window Materials We Reviewed Often Lacked Key Information Participants Need to Make an Informed Decision

Participants need information in certain key areas to make an informed decision about their options when provided a lump sum offer. While our analysis of materials provided by plan sponsors showed that they appeared to include certain required information, they often lacked other key information. Most participants we interviewed cited fear that their sponsor would not deliver on their pension promise as a primary reason for accepting the lump sum offer, but many of these participants were not aware of the protections afforded by PBGC.

Participants Need Information in Eight Key Areas to Make an Informed Decision

Based on a review of publications by federal agencies, the ERISA Advisory Council, financial advisors, investment firms, financial services firms, and participant advocacy groups, as well as relevant federal laws and regulations, we identified eight key areas of information that participants need to weigh their options and determine what is in their best interest when faced with a lump sum window offer (see table 1).

Under existing federal law and regulations, plan sponsors who offer a lump sum in place of a retirement annuity are required to provide certain disclosures to participants related to some of the eight key areas we identified.[79] For example, the sponsors' disclosures to participants are required to include information on the need for spousal consent, the tax implications of taking a lump sum, and the relative value of the lump sum compared with the plan's benefits. However, this information, even when provided as required, may not be sufficient to enable participants to make an informed decision. During the ERISA Advisory Council hearings in 2013, several experts testified about their concerns for participants being offered lump sums. In their testimony, some experts noted that participants may not fully understand their retirement benefits or the risks involved in taking their benefits in the form of a lump sum payment. For example, participants electing a lump sum assume responsibility for investing their retirement assets and thus bear the risk of both market losses and of outliving their retirement assets. The council recommended that the disclosure materials include additional information to clarify, among other things, the tax implications of a lump sum payment, the treatment of early retirement subsidies in the lump sum calculation, and how participants' benefit options compare against each other.

Table 1. Eight Questions that Address Key Factors Participants Need to Know In Order to Make an Informed Benefit Choice

Question addressing key factor	Examples of sub-questions for key factor
1. What benefit options are available?	•What is the monthly benefit amount at normal retirement age (the "do nothing now" or "deferred annuity" option)? •Is there a subsidized early retirement option? •What is the monthly benefit amount if payments begin now under the plan (the "immediate annuity" option)? •What is the lump sum amount (the "lump sum" option)?
2. How was the lump sum calculated?	•What interest rates were used? •What mortality assumptions were used? •Was the value of any additional plan benefits included in the lump sum?

Question addressing key factor	Examples of sub-questions for key factor
3. What is the relative value of the lump sum versus the monthly annuity?[a]	•How does the lump sum payment compare to the value of the plan's lifetime annuity?
	•Would it be possible to replicate the plan's stream of payments by purchasing a retail annuity using the lump sum?
4. What are the potential positive and negative ramifications of accepting the lump sum?	•How could taking the lump sum affect beneficiaries? •How could inflation affect the lump sum and plan's monthly benefits? •What are the investment risks? •What are the longevity risks? •How could spending some of the lump sum affect its value over time?
5. What are the tax implications of accepting a lump sum?[a]	•How would the lump sum payment be taxed? •What rollover options are available and what are the tax implications foreach? •Are there early distribution penalties?
6. What is the role of PBGC and what level of protection does PBGC provide on each benefit option?	•What is PBGC? •How much of the plan's monthly benefit would be protected by PBGC if the plan is terminated with insufficient assets to pay benefits?
7. What are the instructions for either accepting or rejecting the lump sum?[a]	•What needs to be done to make either election? •What is the deadline for the decision? •Does a spouse need to grant consent for either election?
8. Who can be contacted for more information or assistance?	•What is the contact method for questions? •Is federal assistance available?

Source: GAO analysis of 18 publications by federal agencies, the ERISA Advisory Council, financial advisors, investment firms, financial services firms, and participant advocacy groups, as well as federal law and regulation. | GAO-15-74

[a]There are some federal requirements related to the provision of this type of key information to participants who receive a lump sum window offer.

Materials Provided by Sponsors Lacked Key Information That Could Have Helped Participants

In our review and analysis of 11 packets of information that sponsors—representing about 248,000 participant offers—provided to participants regarding a lump sum window offer, we found that all of the packets lacked important information that could have helped participants. However, all packets appeared to include information that is required by current federal law and regulations governing benefit distributions.[80] For example, all packets included a spousal waiver for electing a lump sum and information about the tax implications associated with the participant's decision. In addition, all of the packets included the required relative value statement. Further, one packet GAO reviewed was commendable in that it provided 7 of the 8 key pieces of information GAO identified, and provided several resources beyond this threshold information. Most packets (8 of 11) provided at least 5 of the 8 key pieces of information GAO identified as necessary to make an informed decision. However, our review also revealed that all 11 packets lacked at least one key piece of information a participant would need to make a more fully informed decision about his or her benefit choices, as described below. Our interviews with 33 plan participants revealed they may have lacked key information, as many (13 of 33) told us that more information would have helped them assess whether or not to accept the lump sum.

Key Factor #1: Benefit Options

We found that all the sponsors' packets initially presented at least two benefit options: the lump sum payment and the monthly benefit amount for an immediate annuity.[81] Most packets (9 of 11) also presented a deferred annuity option: the estimated monthly benefit amount promised under the plan once the participant reached the plan's normal retirement age. Only one packet provided the amount of the monthly annuity at the plan's early retirement age.[82] In the cases involving the two packets that did not provide information about a deferred annuity option at normal retirement age, the participants were separated participants who had not begun to receive monthly pension benefits. While some participants might have on file the estimated monthly benefit amount at normal retirement age, others may not.[83] Without that information, it would be challenging for participants to determine if deferring receipt of benefits until reaching normal retirement age should be an option worth considering. One participant we interviewed whose sponsor did not provide this information said that she was glad she had retained records showing her estimated pension amount because otherwise it would have been difficult to assess her lump sum offer effectively.

Participant Quote

"I'm glad I keep my files up to date. It would have been really hard to figure out whether I was being offered a good deal if I hadn't had a copy of what I'd get at retirement if I waited. I don't think it's right I had to dig for this information." – 40-49 year old woman

Source: GAO's interviews with participants. | GAO-15-74

Three participants we interviewed (affiliated with one plan sponsor) were very concerned that their sponsor did not provide information on the estimated monthly benefits that participants could receive once they qualified for an early retirement. According to that plan's provisions, participants who had enough years of employment could receive unreduced monthly benefits as early as age 60 rather than at the normal retirement age of 65. If participants are not informed of this option, they may not realize that they could be eligible to receive the same monthly benefit 5 years sooner.[84]

Participant Quote

"I felt the way the information was presented was very misleading. The packets made it look like you would have to wait to age 65 to receive unreduced benefits, but actually it could be 60. Some people close to age 60 would be much better off waiting a year or two to get full benefits than accepting a lump sum." – 40-49 year old man

Source: GAO's interviews with participants. | GAO-15-74

Key Factor #2: Lump Sum Calculation

With respect to the lump sum calculation, we found that the information in only 2 of the 11 packets fully explained how the lump sum had been generated, providing sufficient information to facilitate an understanding of the interest rate, mortality table, and benefit used by the sponsor. The remaining 9 packets lacked some key information used in calculating the lump sum amount, such as the interest rates or mortality assumptions. For example, 8 of the 11 packets did not disclose the interest rates used for the calculation.[85]

In addition, 7 of the 11 packets lacked information about the specific mortality assumptions used in the calculation. Lastly, 4 packets did not explain whether certain additional plan benefits, such as early retirement subsidies, were included in the calculation. Although not all participants would necessarily use information about interest rates, mortality assumptions, or treatment of additional plan benefits to help them arrive at a decision, our discussions with participants informed us that some (7) likely would.

Participant Quote

"As an engineer with considerable expertise in finance, I found it very frustrating that I could not figure out how my lump sum had been calculated from the information provided. It took me many phone calls to the call center and hours working with a spreadsheet to understand what assumptions were used in calculating my lump sum. I am still not 100 percent sure the calculation was done correctly, but I figure it was close enough." – 60-69 year old man

Source: GAO's interviews with participants. | GAO-15-74

Many participants we questioned either reported that they were not provided the exact interest rates or mortality assumptions (15 of 37), or they found the information that they were provided about interest rate or mortality assumptions confusing (8 of 37). Many participants who were not provided this information (12 of 15) said they wished their plan sponsor had provided it as part of the lump sum offer materials. Specifically, some participants (6 of 15) told us they wanted to know what interest rates or mortality assumptions had been used so they could assess whether the assumptions were fair. Some participants (7 of 15) said they wanted the underlying assumptions and a clearer explanation as to how the lump sum was calculated to confirm it had been calculated correctly.[86] A few of these participants (4 of 15) said they had been able to obtain information on mortality assumptions or interest rates through a call center, and all of these participants said they should not have had to track down this information themselves. For example, one participant said that she had to contact the call center several times before learning she would have to write a formal request to receive the information. This individual believed the information should have been provided clearly in the information materials.

Key Factor #3: Relative Value of a Lump Sum versus an Annuity

In all the packets we reviewed, we found the relative value notice required by IRS to inform participants how the overall value of the lump sum compares to that of the plan's annuity. These statements typically took the form of a table. 87 We found little additional explanation in any of the packets to help participants understand what the numbers meant. Some participants (7 of 33) said the relative value statements were not user friendly or particularly helpful for them in assessing whether to accept the lump sum.

Most (7 of 11) of the packets we reviewed contained relative value statements that showed the lump sum offered had "approximately the same value" as the lifetime annuity provided by the plan when calculated as permitted under current law.88 In two packets, the relative value statement showed that the lump sum payment was less valuable than the annuity. In two other cases, the relative value statement showed that the lump sum payment was actually worth significantly more than the annuity (114 and 120 percent). Plan participants may not understand the importance and effect of assumptions used to calculate the relative values, and the materials we reviewed did not explain why the lump sum values may be more or less valuable than an annuity. In the absence of any further explanation, it is unclear how participants could have interpreted the results or to what extent the notice could help them reach an informed decision.

In addition, in many (5 of 11) of the packets, the relative value statements compared the lump sum payment amount to the value of an immediate annuity starting at the same time as the lump sum payment would occur, but not the value of the deferred annuity available when the participant reached full retirement age, often at age 65.[89] It also was not clear if any of these packets included the value of a deferred annuity beginning at early retirement age with any additional plan benefits.[90] A number of the packets did not disclose whether the participant would be eligible for any additional plan benefits, such as early retirement subsidies, if they waited to claim their annuity (4 of 11). IRS guidance allows sponsors to show a relative value notice for an immediate annuity, which may exclude consideration of certain additional plan benefits that have not yet been earned. However, this may limit the usefulness of the relative value statement for participants, who may be eligible for early retirement benefits at some point in the future or who could qualify for other types of additional plan benefits.[91]

Participant Quote

"I also researched what I could buy in the way of a market annuity to generate a similar benefit and found that the amount of my lump sum offer wasn't nearly enough to replicate the monthly payments I was guaranteed under the pension plan." – 60-69 year old man

Source: GAO's interviews with participants. | GAO-15-74

Further, none of the relative value statements included information about how much it would cost on the open market to replicate the same stream of payments from the plan's lifetime annuity. While there is no obligation for sponsors to do so, and it might not be reasonable to expect sponsors to research the open market to provide such an estimate, many participants trying to assess the relative value of a lump sum could benefit from researching and considering this cost.

Several participants (4 of 33) said they had either researched or asked their financial advisor to estimate how much it would cost to buy a market annuity equal to their promised lifetime annuity. Two others had tried to determine the monthly benefit they would be able to secure if they used their lump sum to purchase a market annuity. After reviewing the figures provided, all 6 participants who analyzed the cost of a market annuity relative to either their plan's monthly annuity benefit or the lump sum amount rejected the lump sum offer.

Key Factor #4: Positive and Negative Ramifications of Accepting a Lump Sum

To make an informed decision about accepting a lump sum, individuals also need to understand potential positive and negative ramifications of their decisions. All 11 of the packets we reviewed discussed at least one of the potential negative ramifications of accepting a lump sum payment, and about half (6) also discussed at least one of the positive ramifications of accepting an offer (see table 2).

A few participants (4 of 33) said that more information related to the positive and negative ramifications would have helped them decide whether or not to accept the lump sum.

Participant Quote

"The materials did not provide much detail about the pros and cons of a lump sum versus an annuity and such information would have been very helpful. The materials I received were very process oriented and did not help me decide whether or not to accept the lump sum." – 50-59 year old man

Source: GAO's interviews with participants. | GAO-15-74

Table 2. Examples of Positive and Negative Ramifications of Accepting a Lump Sum

Potential positive ramifications of accepting a lump sum	Potential inflation protection (depending on investment choices and actual returns)
	Potential to leave a bequest to a beneficiary other than a spouse
	Ability to consolidate retirement assets
	Control over investment decisions
	Possibility of earning investment returns
Potential negative ramifications of accepting a lump sum	Loss of spousal benefits after participant's death
	Participant bears investment risk
	Participant bears responsibility for managing the money
	Participant bears the risk of outliving the lump sum funds (longevity risk)
	Participant bears the risk of overspending (in the absenceof the budgeting signal provided by a monthly pension)

Source: GAO analysis of 18 publications by federal agencies, the ERISA Advisory Council, financial advisors, investment firms, financial services firms, and participant advocacy groups, as well as federal law and regulation. | GAO-15-74

The risk of outliving their assets, or "longevity risk," was of key concern to many participants we interviewed and a primary reason cited for rejecting a lump sum offer. Specifically, of the 22 participants who completed our questionnaire and who had chosen to reject the lump sum, the most common reason cited for this decision (17) was concern about the possibility that they would run out of money before they died if they took the lump sum. Most participants (24 of 33) told us they had tried to estimate how long they would have to live to break even with the lump sum offer,[92] and many of those who rejected the lump sum (10 of 22) pointed to their own good health or long-lived relatives as reasons to keep their plan's lifetime annuity.

Participant Quote

"I used a projection that I would live to be 85. Based on that, the lump sum payout fell short. As long as I collected for 20 years or more I would be better off sticking with the annuity." – 60-69 year old man

Source: GAO's interviews with participants. | GAO-15-74

A number of participants we interviewed expressed their desire to gain control of how their retirement savings were invested or bequeathed. For example, a few participants (3 of 15) expressed their appreciation of the lump sum because it gave them the ability to control and manage the monies themselves. Likewise, a few participants (3 of 15) elected the lump sum because they wanted to be able to leave money to a beneficiary other than a spouse when they die. For instance, one woman wanted to ensure that her daughter would benefit from the pension funds, and one man we interviewed lived in a state that did not recognize same-sex marriages at the time the lump sum offer was made and wanted to ensure his partner would be able to access the funds.[93]

Participant Quote

I feel better [taking the lump sum] knowing my investment is in a 401(k) plan rather than the company sponsored [defined benefit] pension. – 40-49 year old woman

Source: GAO's interviews with participants. | GAO-15-74

Participants' understanding of the positive and negative ramifications of accepting a lump sum offer would be enhanced to the extent the participants have adequate levels of financial literacy (combined with adequate disclosure of information as discussed above). For example, understanding the risk of outliving one's assets could help participants make a more informed decision. In addition, for participants who do elect a lump sum, financial literacy could help with the challenges of managing that lump sum. Participants' elections are also influenced by factors other than rational analysis of benefits and risks.[94] Adequate disclosure, combined with financial literacy, could potentially help counteract behavioral tendencies that sometimes might not result in the best outcomes for participants.

Participant Quote

"I am divorced with a grown daughter. I accepted the lump sum because I wanted to be sure she would at least get something if I was hit by a bus tomorrow." – 50-59 year old woman

Source: GAO's interviews with participants. | GAO-15-74

Key Factor #5: Tax Implications

Participant Quote

"The materials on the tax implications were clear, but I wish it had been possible to roll the funds directly into an IRA rather than have the added headache of receiving a check and having to transfer the funds myself. It was a bit nerve wracking because I didn't want to take a hit if I did something wrong with such a big amount of money." – 50-59 year old man

Source: GAO's interviews with participants. | GAO-15-74

Individuals must also understand the tax implications of accepting a lump sum in order to make an informed decision. All 11 of the election packets we reviewed outlined the tax implications of accepting a lump sum. Specifically, each packet presented information about rollover options and their tax implications. In addition, each election packet disclosed that participants under the age of 591/2 could be subject to early distribution penalties if they elected a lump sum payment and did not roll the funds into a qualified retirement account. About half the individuals who filled out our questionnaire (20 of 37) said they felt that the information provided to them about the tax implications of their decision was understandable, and almost all the individuals who accepted a lump sum rolled it into an IRA.[95]

Key Factor #6: PBGC Protection

To make an informed decision regarding lump sums, individuals also need to assess the risk that a plan might not have sufficient funds to fully make promised payments, and understand the extent to which their promised pension would be guaranteed by PBGC if that were to happen. Indeed, most participants we interviewed (10 of 15) who accepted lump sums said that one of the main reasons they chose to accept the lump sum was because they were worried the sponsor would default on its pension promise.[96] Further, only 2 of the 11 election packets we reviewed explained the role of PBGC or provided information on the level of PBGC protections to an individual's lifetime annuity. Our discussions with individuals offered lump sum payments suggest that many of them could have benefited from knowing more about PBGC and the level of pension protection it offers. [97] Of the 15 participants who completed our questionnaire and had chosen the lump sum, most (10) said that one of the primary reasons they elected the lump sum was they were worried the plan would default on its pension promise and they could lose some or all of their benefits. Many of these individuals (6 of 10) were not aware of the protections offered by PBGC.

Pension Benefit Guaranty Corporation (PBGC) Protections

PBGC is a government corporation created by the Employee Retirement Income Security Act of 1974 (ERISA) to protect pension benefits in private defined benefit plans. When plans insured by PBGC end—known as a plan termination—without enough money to pay all benefits, PBGC's single-employer insurance program pays participants the benefit they would have received from their pension plan up to certain limits set by law. PBGC's maximum benefit guarantee is set each year under ERISA. The maximum guarantee applicable to a plan is generally fixed as of that plan's termination date. For 2014, the maximum guaranteed amount for singe-employer plans is about $59,320 per year for workers who begin receiving payments from PBGC at age 65. The maximum guarantee is lower for participants who begin receiving payments from PBGC before age 65, or if the pension includes benefits for a surviving spouse or other beneficiary. The maximum benefit is higher for participants who are over age 65 when they begin receiving benefits. In addition, PBGC's guaranteed benefit amounts are subject to the "phase-in" limit (related to benefit increases made in the previous 5 years) and the "accrued-at-normal" limit (which excludes supplemental benefits).

> Participants can find out whether their pension plan is insured by PBGC by obtaining a copy of the plan's "Summary Plan Description," or SPD, from the employer or plan administrator. A table showing PBGC's maximum guarantee at various ages can be found at http://www.pbgc.gov/wr/benefits/guaranteed-benefits/maximum-guarantee.html.

Source: PBGC, "Your Guaranteed Pension," http://www.pbgc.gov/wr /benefits guaranteed-benefits/your-guaranteed-pension.html.

The other participants (4 of 10) were aware of PBGC's protections, but said they were worried they would not receive their full benefit or any benefit at all from PBGC if their pension plan defaulted. Specifically, a few individuals we interviewed (3 of 15) told us that they had accepted the lump sum—even though they believed it to be a bad deal—because they were afraid they might ultimately be left with nothing if their plan sponsor went out of business or mishandled the pension funds. For example, one participant said he was afraid he would "walk away with nothing," and another said he was concerned he would "only get pennies on the dollar." Yet another participant said he had decided to "get out while the going is good."

> **Participant Quote**
>
> "I was very concerned about what I saw as the mismanagement of the company, so I decided I had better take the money and run." – 50-59 year old woman
>
> Source: GAO's interviews with participants. | GAO-15-74

Key Factors #7 and #8: Instructions and Assistance

Understanding how to complete the administrative process of making a benefit election and who to contact for help are two other important pieces of information plan participants need in order to make an informed decision. All 11 of the election material packets we reviewed provided clear administrative instructions on how to elect a lump sum, immediate annuity, or deferred annuity. Similarly, all packets provided a contact, such as a call center, for asking general questions about the lump sum offer. In addition, almost all the plan sponsors provided contact information for at least one source of federal assistance, typically the IRS.

Participants responding to our questionnaire generally did not raise concerns related to the administrative steps needed to elect a lump sum or retain their annuity, or the length of time they had to make their decision. Specifically, most said the data included in the election materials (such as years of service and age) were accurate (29 of 37) and that they found the process of completing the paperwork fairly straightforward (23 of 37). Few (2 of 37) reported experiencing significant administrative burdens in gathering the required information (identification, notarized consents, etc).

Participant Quote

"Overall I think my sponsor did a good job of putting together very professional and helpful materials. I found the spreadsheet where I could adjust assumptions particularly helpful. I'm grateful they did such a good job providing information to help me make my decision, and I hope other employers do as well by their former employees." –70-plus year old man

Source: GAO's interviews with participants. | GAO-15-74

Fear of Plan Default and of Outliving Assets Were Cited As Main Reasons for Accepting or Rejecting a Lump Sum Offer

A few themes emerged regarding the primary reasons participants who completed our questionnaire either accepted or rejected their lump sum offer, and how they went about making their decisions (see figure 3). Specifically, most participants accepting the lump sum offer were motivated by fear that retaining their annuity would hurt their prospects for a secure retirement (10 of 15), either because the pension plan would default on its promise (10 of 15) or because the plan sponsor would not manage the pension benefits responsibly (6 of 15).[98] In contrast, many participants who chose to reject the lump sum offer indicated that their retirement might be more secure if they retained their annuity.

Specifically, most of these participants (17 of 22) did not think the lump sum amount would last as long as they expected to live and a majority (14 of 22) believed that the calculation was unfair or not to their benefit.

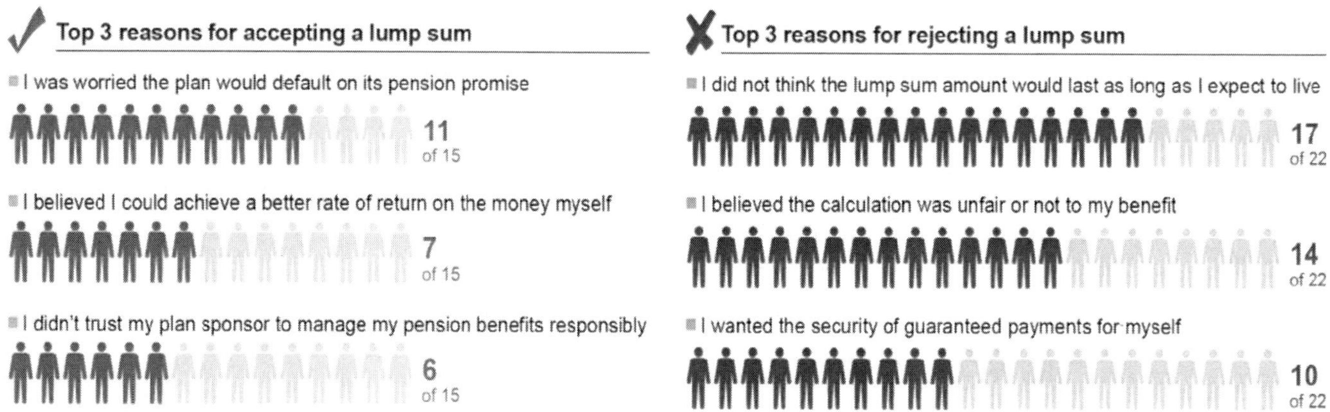

Source: Analysis of GAO participant-questionnaire data. | GAO-15-74

Figure 3. Top Three Reasons Cited by Participants for Accepting or Rejecting a Lump Sum.

Participant Quote

"I trust my financial advisor who has been managing my money for over 15 years. I brought him everything to make sure I wasn't missing anything." –50-59 year old man

Source: GAO's interviews with participants. | GAO-15-74.

Most participants (27 of 37) reported taking at least three steps to assess whether or not to accept the lump sum. Specifically, most participants reported conducting research using the Internet and reading articles about lump sum offers. Many participants (20) also reported trying to estimate the lump sum's value based on anticipated life expectancy and using various interest rates. About a third of participants (11 of 37) reported receiving a tool from their sponsor—such as a spreadsheet or calculator—they could use to assess the lump sum offer and of those, many (7 of 11) said it was very helpful. Two participants who did not receive such a tool from their sponsor said they wished they had. Most (30 of 37) participants also consulted with professionals, such as financial advisors or tax professionals, to help them assess the lump sum offer. About a quarter of participants (9 of 37) reported receiving unsolicited contacts by individuals not formally connected with the pension plan while trying to decide whether to accept the lump sum.

CONCLUSION

While plan sponsors may be permitted by law to choose to offer their participants lump sum windows to reduce the financial risks associated with their defined benefit plans, the full extent of their use is unknown. It is apparent that lump sum windows affect a significant number of plan participants and can involve very large amounts of lump sum payments. Some of the recent lump sum window offers may have been driven by federal rules that may serve as cost-saving incentives for sponsors to take such actions. Through lump sum payments, sponsors transfer the risks and responsibility of retirement security away from themselves—and the defined benefit system more generally—and onto participants. As the proportion of the U.S. population over age 65 increases, the importance of retirement security for our country's well-being increases as well. Yet the federal agencies charged with pension oversight have not been able to fully examine how these risk transfers impact workers and retirees— and thus cannot take steps to ensure any potential adverse effects on participants are minimized.

Given the likelihood that plan sponsors will continue to use lump sum window offers as a means of reducing current pension liabilities, we share a number of the 2013 ERISA Advisory Council's concerns about these risk transfers. For example, the pension oversight agencies lack data about when and where these actions occur, who is affected, and how these actions impact participants. This means that the agencies may not have sufficient information to determine whether additional participant protections are needed when sponsors implement lump sum windows.

For participants being asked to choose between a lifetime benefit option and a lump sum, it is important that they understand how the two compare. As our analyses show, once a participant cashes out a lifetime annuity by taking a lump sum, the participant's retirement savings can be diminished in a number of ways or used on other expenses. Participants may not be aware of the effect that certain allowable assumptions used to determine their lump sum—such as outdated mortality tables and favorable "lookback" interest rates—may have on their ultimate payment amount. In most cases, the lump sum payment received is unlikely to purchase an equivalent annuity on the retail annuity market. Furthermore, the lump sum is exposed to potential erosion over the years, as the participant assumes all the risks inherent in managing both the investment and drawdown of their lump sum amount. Regrettably, such challenges may become more acute as the participant ages and the effort required for sound financial management becomes more burdensome. Ultimately, the greatest risk associated with accepting a lump sum is the risk of outliving it, which may occur despite the most savvy management.

Participants presented with a lump sum offer may not have a full appreciation of the range of risks involved in forfeiting their lifetime annuity under their sponsor's plan. While we found that some sponsors did a commendable job in their efforts to inform participants about their benefit choices, it is notable that such efforts often fell short of fully preparing the participant to make an informed decision based on many of the eight key factors we identified. The relative value statements were often confusing, explanations of how the lump sum was calculated were often lacking, and many participants did not understand the PBGC protections they would be giving up by taking a lump sum.

RECOMMENDATIONS FOR EXECUTIVE ACTION

To ensure that federal regulators have better information about lump sum windows and to better ensure that participants have ready access to key information they need to make a decision when presented with a lump sum offer, the Department of Labor should:

1) Require plan sponsors to notify DOL at the time they implement a lump sum window offer, including the number and category of participants being extended the offer (e.g., separated vested; retiree) as well as examples of the materials provided to them.
2) Coordinate with IRS and PBGC to clarify the guidance regarding the information sponsors should provide to participants when extending lump sum window offers and place the guidance on the agency's website. Guidance should include clear and understandable presentations of information, such as the relative value of the lump sum, the role and level of protections provided by PBGC, and the positive and negative ramifications of accepting the lump sum. Such guidance could also include promising practices for information materials from plan sponsors which are particularly effective in facilitating informed participant decision-making.

In addition, to provide participants with useful information and to provide for lump sums that are based on up-to-date assumptions, Treasury should:

1) Review its regulations governing the information contained in relative value statements to ensure these statements provide a meaningful comparison of all benefit options, especially in instances where the loss of certain additional plan benefits may not be disclosed.
2) Review the applicability and appropriateness of allowing sponsors to select a "lookback" interest rate for use in calculating lump sums associated with a lump sum window that can serve to advantage the interests of the sponsor.
3) Establish a process and a timeline for periodically updating the mortality tables used to determine minimum required lump sums—including a means for monitoring when experts' views may indicate that mortality tables may have become outdated, and for taking expedited action if warranted.

AGENCY COMMENTS

We provided a draft of this report to DOL, Treasury (including IRS), and PBGC for their review and comment. Treasury and PBGC did not provide written comments.

DOL provided written comments. DOL, Treasury (on behalf of IRS) and PBGC provided technical comments, which we incorporated where appropriate. In oral comments, Treasury officials generally agreed with our recommendations.

In its written comments, DOL generally agreed with the findings and conclusions of the report. They noted the challenges participants may face when they take on the risks of pension management themselves. Specifically, DOL noted that EBSA is especially committed to increasing awareness of lifetime income options because participants are increasingly taking on many retirement management responsibilities. GAO agrees that increasing awareness of lifetime income options in retirement is a worthy goal. Additionally, understanding the scope of lump sum window offers and the informational needs participants have under such offers could help focus efforts to educate participants on the importance of lifetime income options at the point of decision.

DOL generally agreed with the recommendations of the report. Specifically, they agreed that the type of information that would be collected pursuant to our first recommendation would be helpful in determining the extent to which lump sum window offers are made and the types of disclosures participants receive.

However, DOL noted that ERISA does not clearly grant the department the authority to impose such a requirement on plan sponsors and said that it will be necessary for EBSA to determine whether DOL has such authority.

We agree that DOL should determine whether there is any action it could take within the scope of its existing authority to implement this recommendation.

Should DOL conclude as a result of its analysis that the department lacks authority to require plan sponsors to notify the department at the time they implement a lump sum window, we would encourage DOL to pursue appropriate legislative changes.

DOL agreed with the second recommendation on coordinating with Treasury (including IRS) and PBGC to clarify guidance regarding information sponsors should provide to participants when extending a lump sum window offer. They noted the manner of publishing such guidance would depend on the coordination process with IRS and PBGC.

Sincerely yours,
Charles A. Jeszeck
Director, Education, Workforce, and Income Security Issues

APPENDIX I: OBJECTIVES, SCOPE, AND METHODOLOGY

Our objectives were to examine 1) the extent to which sponsors of defined benefit plans are transferring risk through the use of lump sum windows, and the incentives for sponsors to take such actions, 2) the implications for participants who accept a lump sum payment, and 3) the extent to which sponsors' lump sum window informational materials enable participants to make an informed decision. To address these objectives we collected and analyzed available information about pension risk transfers. We also interviewed managers from three plan sponsors and other stakeholders, such as consultants, insurance company representatives, independent fiduciaries, and subject matter experts. In addition, we administered a questionnaire to plan participants, interviewed selected participants, and collected and analyzed disclosure materials given to participants. We developed a lump sum calculator to analyze lump sum calculations. Lastly, we reviewed literature, as well as federal laws and regulations relevant to pension risk transfers. We conducted this performance audit from March 2013 to January 2015 in accordance with generally accepted government auditing standards. Those standards require that we plan and perform the audit to obtain sufficient, appropriate evidence to provide a reasonable basis for our findings and conclusions based on our audit objectives. We believe that the evidence obtained provides a reasonable basis for our findings and conclusions based on our audit objectives.

Literature Review and Legal Analysis

We reviewed literature, laws, and regulations relevant to risk transfer activities. Most literature was obtained from ERISA Advisory Council testimonies, pension expert and consultant presentations, and other materials obtained during pension-related conferences, as well as publications and whitepapers issued by subject matter experts, pension-related organizations, business associations, consulting firms, and insurance companies. Legal research primarily focused on the Employee Retirement Income Security Act of 1974 (ERISA), Pension Protection Act of 2006 (PPA), Moving Ahead for Progress in the 21st Century Act (MAP-21), and the Internal Revenue Code, but also included additional research on laws and regulations governing retirement income, benefit distributions, and participant disclosures.

Data Collection for Pension Risk Transfer Actions

We used a variety of sources to collect information about recent pension risk transfer actions that U.S. plan sponsors have taken. Prior to identifying these actions, we asked relevant federal agency officials and pension experts what sources of information were available and we were told such sources were limited. To identify sponsors who had implemented a lump sum window during 2012, we first used lists provided to us by the Pension Benefit Guaranty Corporation (PBGC) officials and the Pension Rights Center. We verified the lists to the extent possible, primarily with information contained in sponsors' SEC filings and corporate reports. We removed sponsors from the lists if we could not find sufficient evidence that they had performed a lump sum window during 2012.

We made efforts to contact managers associated with 18 risk transfer actions in order to collect additional information and schedule interviews. For all but three sponsors, we either were not able to establish contact with the appropriate manager, the sponsor was unresponsive to our efforts, or we were told that the sponsor did not wish to participate in our study. During the interviews with the three sponsors who agreed to speak with us, we asked questions regarding the lump sum window implementation process they followed, the reasons behind their decision to transfer pension risk, and to the extent possible, the outcomes of the action. In some cases, we also collected informational materials that had been provided to participants offered lump sums.

To supplement the sponsor interviews, we interviewed other stakeholders, such as pension consultants, insurance company representatives, an independent fiduciary, and subject matter experts. We asked them about several aspects related to lump sum offers, such as recent trends, what is driving the practice, and their potential effect on plan participants. We also reviewed written reports, papers, and studies conducted by consulting firms and other pension experts to gain a better understanding about the prevalence of pension risk transfers, in general, and why sponsors may be conducting or considering them.

Data Collection for Participant Disclosure Materials and Participant Experiences

To collect information to provide the participant perspective of lump sum windows, we first used social media to identify corporate alumni groups associated with the sponsors we had identified as having offered lump sums during 2012. From those groups we solicited participants who had been offered lump sums and received over 65 responses from participants who were interested in participating in our study. From those, we selected 37 participants across as many sponsors as possible. To those individuals we administered a questionnaire that asked them to provide information on their overall experience when offered a lump sum, what they considered when making their decision, their opinion on the understandability and usefulness of the information packet they had received from the sponsor, and why they ultimately made the choice they did. We also conducted phone interviews with 33 of the 37 participants in order to gain additional insight into their questionnaire responses, and to supplement the information captured by the instrument. We did not independently verify information presented by participants in these interviews. Consequently, no legal conclusions can be drawn from our work as to whether plan sponsors complied with any applicable legal requirements.

Our selection of participants to survey was also designed to yield a group of participants that represented a relatively broad variety of attributes, such as gender, age, and whether they had accepted the lump sum offer or not. The selected participants represented 11 different sponsors. Most of these individuals were ages 50 to 59, with the remaining individuals fairly evenly split between the 40 to 49 and 60 to 69 year old age groups. Almost all the participants had been salaried employees. Most individuals in the survey group were currently working full time. Most, including those who were working and those who were fully retired, had other sources of retirement income in addition to the defined benefit plan for which they were offered a lump sum, including Individual Retirement Accounts, 401(k) or 403(b) plans, and Social Security benefits. Of these 37 participants, 15 accepted the lump sum offer and 22 rejected the lump sum offer. While not generalizable, we used the participants' responses from the questionnaires and phone interviews to inform our discussion about the factors participants weighed when making their benefit choices.

In addition, we developed a lump sum calculator to generate lump sum amounts based on participant information obtained during our interviews, such as age, gender, and deferred annuity amount. Using the calculator, we mimicked sponsor lump sum calculations to gain a better understanding of how mandated assumptions affect lump sum amounts, and how changes in those assumptions affected amounts for participants across differing ages and gender. For details of those analyses, see appendix II.

Factors for Analyzing Packets

During participant interviews we asked participants if they could provide us the written materials that sponsors gave them when offering the lump sum. We asked participants to redact any personally identifiable information such as names or offer amounts, and asked for as many materials as they could provide. Because these materials were participant-provided, we cannot be certain whether the materials we reviewed were accurate and complete representations of the materials provided by each sponsor to its affected participants. Similarly, participants provided us materials in hardcopy, so, for example, materials that sponsors provided electronically might not have been transmitted to GAO unless the participant had printed and retained this information. Electronic information likely would have been password protected and not available for GAO's review. We collected at least one packet for each of the 11 sponsors executing lump sum offers to the participants we interviewed. These 11 sponsors represent, according to our review of SEC filings, about 248,000 participant offers.

To analyze participant packets, we identified eight key areas of information participants would need to understand in order to make an informed decision about a lump sum offer.[1] To identify these areas, we gathered information from federal agencies, the ERISA Advisory Council, financial advisors, investment firms, financial services firms, participant advocacy groups, and federal laws and regulations. Since these key factors were gathered from diverse sources, they were also vetted and reviewed by GAO's Chief Actuary and a research methodologist to ensure they could be applied when we analyzed the materials for informational content.

To apply the eight key factors to the informational materials, we identified specific pieces of information, or sub-factors, that the packet would need to contain in order to fully satisfy the main factor. GAO developed decision rules for each main factor regarding how many of these sub-factors were needed in order to fully satisfy the main factor. Under these decision rules, for seven of the eight key factors, all sub-factors needed to be present to fully satisfy the main factor. However, for one of the eight factors, our decision rule only required that one of the elements be present. Specifically, for our factor on "What are the potential positive and negative ramifications of accepting the lump sum?," we identified many potential positive or negative ramifications that could be highlighted in the materials, but specified that a packet only need to list at least one negative ramification of accepting the lump sum to satisfy this factor. Table 3 has more detail on the extent to which the packets, in aggregate, met our main factors and sub-factors.

Table 3. Overview of GAO's Informational Review of 11 Lump Sum Offer Packets

Key questions participants need answered in order to make an informed decision	Number of packets fully answering these key questions[a]	The specific details GAO looked for to assess if the packets included the information necessary to answer the key questions [and the number of packets containing those details][a]
1. What benefit options are available?	9	•Amount of the lump sum offer [all 11] •Amount of the deferred annuity,starting at normal retirement age for terminated vested participants; or the current annuity payment,for participants already in pay status [9 of 11] •Amount of the immediate annuity,for terminated vested participants; or alternate annuity form,for participants already in pay status [all 11]
2. How was the lump sum calculated?	2	•Mortality assumptionsused in calculating the lump-sum clearly shown [4 of 11] •Interest rates used and their effect on the lump sum amount [3 of 11]

Key questions participants need answered in order to make an informed decision	Number of packets fully answering these key questions[a]	The specific details GAO looked for to assess if the packets included the information necessary to answer the key questions [and the number of packets containing those details][a]
		•Whether any additional plan benefits were included in the calculation ornot [5 of 11]
3. What is the relative value of the lump sum versus the monthly annuity (both immediate and deferred)?	0	•Relative value notice[all 11] •Difference between an annuity, or stream of payments, and a lump-sum is explained clearly [all 11] •Concept of present value clearly explained [3 of 11] •Discussed fact that it might cost more than the lump-sum amount to buy the current annuity benefits on the open market [0 of 11]
4. What are the potential positive and negative ramifications of accepting the lump sum?	11	•Potential positive ramifications discussed[6 of 11] •Potential negative ramificationsdiscussed [all 11]
5. What are the tax implications of accepting a lump sum?	11	•Rollover options and their tax implications presented[all 11] •Potential early distribution penalties discussed [all 11]
6. What is the role of the Pension Benefit Guaranty Corporation and what level of protection does PBGC provide for each benefit option?	2	•PBGC protectionsdiscussed[2 of 11] •Maximum level of PBGC protectionsdiscussed [2 of 11]
7. How do I accept or reject the lump sum offer?	11	•Instructions for making a lump sum electionpresented clearly[all 11] •Instructions for electing an immediate annuity or a new form of annuitypresented clearly [all 11] •Instructions for electing to keep the deferred annuityor current annuity payments presented clearly [all 11]

Table 3. (Continued)

Key questions participants need answered in order to make an informed decision	Number of packets fully answering these key questions[a]	The specific details GAO looked for to assess if the packets included the information necessary to answer the key questions [and the number of packets containing those details][a]
		•Deadlines for making an electionpresented clearly [all 11] •Instructions make it clear that a spouse must grant consentin order to elect to receive a lump sum [all 11]
8. Where can I get more information or assistance?	9	•Contact method provided for general questions[all 11] •Source for federal assistanceprovided [9 of 11]

Source: GAO analysis of 11 lump sum offer packets using eight GAO factors developed from a GAO analysis of 18 publications by federal agencies, the ERISA Advisory Council, financial advisors, investment firms, financial services firms, and participant advocacy groups, as well as federal law and regulation. | GAO-15-74

[a]Our limited review of these materials did not constitute a compliance review, so we did not reach any determinations as to whether individual sponsors complied with any applicable legal requirements in providing materials to their participants. Accordingly, the numbers presented in these columns cannot be read as indicating that any plan sponsors either complied with or failed to comply with any applicable legal requirements.

As noted earlier, this review was an information review and did not constitute a compliance or legal review. Our only purpose in conducting this review was to determine whether the information packets provided to participants in connection with lump sum offers contained sufficient information to enable them to make informed decisions. Consequently, no legal conclusions can be drawn from our work as to whether plan sponsors complied with any applicable legal requirements. As with the development of these factors for analyzing the information packets, the process for implementing the factors was vetted and reviewed by GAO's Chief Actuary and a research methodologist. An analyst reviewed the materials for informational content based on the implementation sub-factors and a second, independent analyst verified the process and validated determinations of the review.

APPENDIX II: LUMP SUM CALCULATIONS AND ADDITIONAL FIGURES

Basic Components of the Lump Sum Calculation

At the most basic level, determining a lump sum is converting a stream of projected future monthly benefits into a present value. A present value is the current worth of a future sum of money or stream of cash flows given a specified rate of return, also known as an interest rate or discount rate. The future cash flows are discounted at the discount rate, and the higher the discount rate, the lower the present value.[1] In the context of a monthly benefit provided by a defined benefit pension plan, the stream of payments generally commences at an age specified by the plan, known as the normal retirement age, or at an optional early retirement age for eligible participants, and ends when the participant dies (or when the later of the participant and beneficiary dies, for a joint annuity).[2] How long the stream of benefits will last depends on how long the participant lives, and lump sums take into account the probability that the participant will be alive at each future date. A mortality table is a common actuarial convention which shows, for each age, the probability that a person will die before his or her next birthday.[3]

Section 417(e)(3) of the Internal Revenue Code (26 U.S.C. § 417(e)(3)),[4] together with regulatory guidance, specifies the interest rates and mortality tables for determining the minimum present value of an annuity, and thus the minimum value of a lump sum. Specifically, the interest rates are published by the Internal Revenue Service (IRS), with the Pension Protection Act of 2006 (PPA) requiring that minimum lump sums be calculated using three different corporate interest rates based on segments of a corporate bond yield curve.[5] The first segment is a short-term corporate bond interest rate applied to projected pension payments payable within 5 years; the second segment is a medium-term corporate bond interest rate applied to payments payable 5 years or more, but less than 20 years, into the future; and the third segment is a long-term corporate bond interest rate applied to payments payable in 20 years or more.

Description of Our Lump Sum Calculations

We constructed a calculator of minimum lump sums to show some of the effect certain methods and assumptions can have on the calculation. We constructed a number of illustrative individuals to show how the minimum lump sums may vary according to key participant characteristics, namely age, gender, and retirement age, and key input calculation parameters, namely interest rates, mortality tables, and the inclusion or exclusion of certain additional plan benefits. While we performed lump sum calculations across a number of illustrative individuals, throughout this appendix we present the results for single individuals in 10-year age increments, from age 35 to age 95. We assumed all individuals are full integer ages—that is, the participant has his or her birthday on the measurement date of the lump sum offer. For terminated vested participants, we assumed a normal retirement age of 65. For retired participants, the present value of their lump sum is calculated and commences at their current age and is based on the remaining payments that are expected to be due from that point forward. Technically, our calculator projects an annual lump sum factor, which produced a lump sum based on an annual benefit. We used a common actuarial adjustment factor to account for monthly payments.

We verified our lump sum calculations in two ways. First, when we started our study we asked Pension Benefit Guaranty Corporation (PBGC) officials with actuarial expertise to furnish us with lump sum amounts based on varying age and benefit commencement assumptions using various mortality and interest rate assumptions consistent with § 417(e)(3).[6] We were able to replicate their calculations, as we planned to base our calculations on annual benefit amounts, and asked the officials to perform the calculation using such a method. Additionally, to determine if we could come reasonably close to actual offers, we reviewed lump sum offers in two participant packets for which we had enough information to calculate or approximate the lump sum in that packet. Our calculations differed by 1.5 percent and nearly zero percent for the two offers we reviewed. The 1.5 percent difference is very modest and may be due to the fact that the birth date or the date of normal retirement age of the participant we used differed from the date of the offer by a few calendar months. Based on these small differences, and since our purpose was to then estimate changes to lump sums based on changes in certain assumptions, we deemed our calculator to be adequate for such purposes.

Figures and Results

We discuss our lump sum results below and show how values can change depending on certain key factors. Generally, we are comparing alternative assumptions to our baseline assumptions. We found, of the materials we reviewed, that many of the lump sum election windows occurred between September and December 2012. Based on our review of election materials, we found that many of these sponsors elected to use August 2011 interest rates for the 2012 plan year. Thus, our "baseline" assumption is an offer made in October 2012, using a methodology under § 417(e)(3) for August 2011 interest rates for the 2012 plan year, along with the IRS published unisex mortality table for the 2012 plan year, and without including any additional plan benefits. Comparisons and deviations from this baseline are noted with the figures.

Figure 4 compares, for our range of ages, the PPA interest rate basis (our baseline) against the pre-PPA interest rate basis for minimum lump sums, for a lump sum payment offer made in October 2012. As noted, our baseline uses August 2011 corporate bond segment rates (for the 2012 plan year), which under PPA uses corporate bond rates published by IRS as the interest rate used to determine minimum required lump sums. The comparison uses the August 2011 30-year Treasury Securities Rate (TSR), as the 30-year TSR was used to determine minimum required lump sums prior to PPA. Figure 4 shows that lump sum payments are most disparate for younger individuals. This occurs because these individuals have their payments discounted at the second or third segment rates, which are much higher than the 30-year TSR in this instance, and because lump sum amounts for younger participants are more sensitive to changes in interest rates because of the greater length of the discounting period. As shown, minimum lump sums for 35-year-old participants would have increased by 142 percent if an August 2011 30- year TSR was used instead of the baseline.

Figure 5 compares the effect of using the "lookback" interest rates that sponsors are allowed to select (our August 2011 interest rates baseline used for the 2012 plan year) against using interest rates as of the month immediately preceding the month of the lump sum offer (September 2012 rates). As noted previously, sponsors may elect a stability period of one year with a maximum lookback of 5 months. This means that the rates used at the time of the offer may be nearly 17 months old compared to rates that are current just before the offer. As shown, minimum lump sums would have been higher at all ages, as much as 65 percent higher for 35-year-olds, if more current interest rates were used instead of the "lookback" rates.

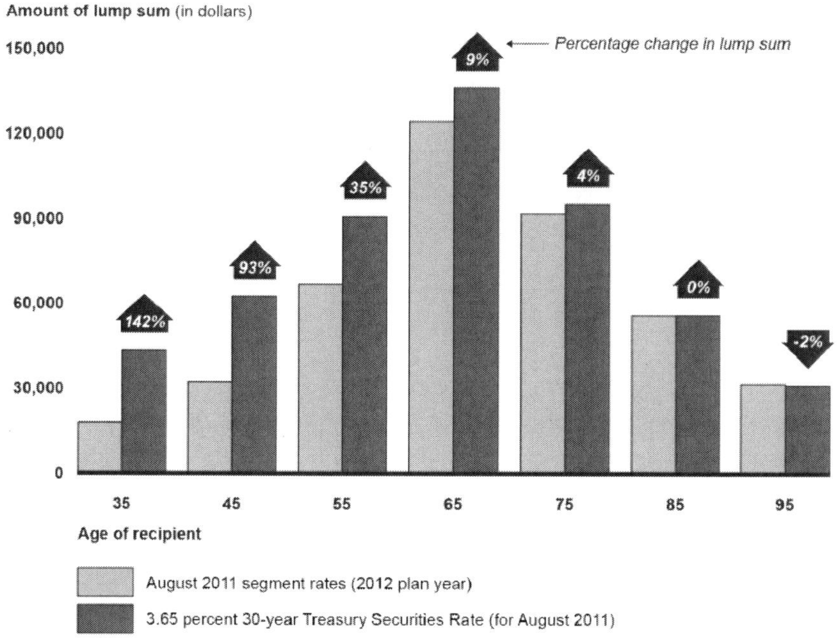

Source: GAO analysis of U.S. Department of the Treasury (Internal Revenue Service) data. | GAO-15-74

Note: Analysis assumes a $10,000 annual benefit (or $833 monthly). The annuity begins at the normal retirement age of 65, for those below age 65. For those older than age 65, the participant is assumed to be in receipt of benefits and thus participant's lump sum is determined using their current age. The August 2011 corporate bond segment rates (for the 2012 plan year) for payments due in less than 5 years, 5 to 20 years, or more than 20 years are 1.85, 4.62, and 6.02 percent, respectively. The August 2011 30-year Treasury Securities Rate is 3.65 percent. Both scenarios use the 2012 mortality table under § 417(e)(3).

Figure 4. PPA Interest Rates Compared to Pre-PPA Interest Rates at Selected Ages, with Lump Sum Payment Based on a $10,000 Annual Benefit Due at Age 65.

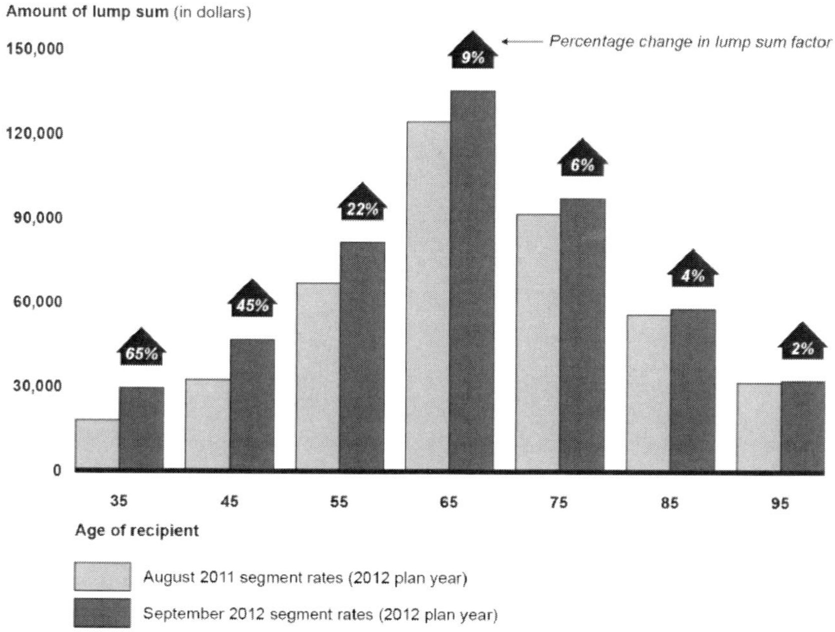

Source: GAO analysis of U.S. Department of the Treasury (Internal Revenue Service) data. | GAO-15-74

Note: Analysis assumes a $10,000 annual benefit (or $833 monthly). The annuity begins at the normal retirement age of 65, for those below age 65. For those offers made at or after age 65, the participant is already receiving the annuity and the lump sum is calculated at the participant's current age. The August 2011 corporate bond segment rates (assumed lookback rates used for the 2012 plan year) for payments due in less than 5 years, 5 to 20 years, or more than 20 years are 1.85, 4.62, and 6.02 percent respectively (baseline). The alternative scenario uses the corporate bond segment rates as of September 2012, which is the month preceding the lump sum offer in this scenario. The September 2012 interest rates are 1.02, 3.71, and 4.67 percent. Both scenarios use the 2012 mortality table under § 417(e)(3).

Figure 5. Effect of "Lookback" Rates on Lump Sum Payments at Selected Ages, with Payment Based on a $10,000 Annual Benefit Due at Age 65.

Figure 6 compares the effect of using current prescribed mortality tables (baseline) against using more up-to-date mortality tables on a participant's minimum lump sum amount at selected ages. Here we show lump sums that are calculated using the new mortality tables and projection scales devised by the Retirement Planning Experience Committee of the Society of Actuaries and compare that to the current mortality tables used for lump sum payments under § 417(e)(3).[7] The differences in lump sum values, which are also sensitive to the assumed interest rate, vary significantly depending on the age of the participant. As shown, the more up-to-date mortality method improves lump sums by as little as 5 percent for 95-year-olds but as much as 13 percent for 35-yearolds.

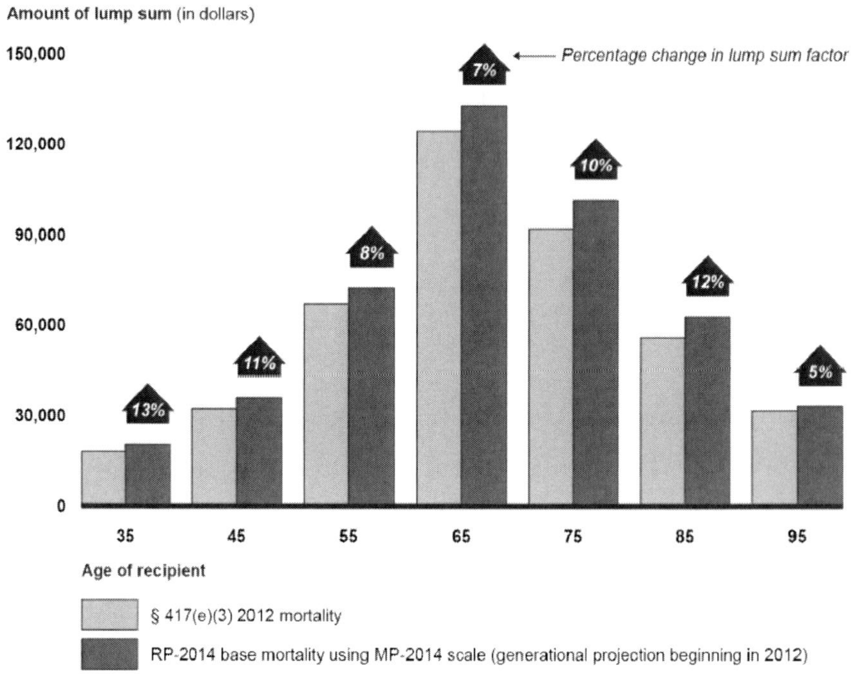

Source: GAO analysis of U.S. Department of the Treasury (Internal Revenue Service) and Society of Actuaries (Retirement Plan Experience Committee, MP-2014 and RP-2014 final reports). | GAO-15-74

Note: Analysis assumes a $10,000 annual benefit (or $833 monthly). The annuity begins at the normal retirement age of 65, for those below age 65. For those offers made at or after age 65, the participant is already receiving the annuity and the lump sum is calculated at the participant's current age. Both lump sum payments use the same August 2011 interest rates (for the 2012 plan year) of 1.85, 4.62, and 6.02 percent.

Figure 6. Effect of Current versus Future Mortality Tables, with Payment Based on a $10,000 Annual Benefit Due at Age 65.

Figure 7 compares baseline lump sums against an estimate of what they would be if based on group annuity purchase rates. It shows how a lump sum payment, calculated in 2012 using sponsor-elected August 2011 corporate bond interest rates (for the 2012 plan year) and the prescribed mortality tables, would compare to lump sum payments calculated in the month before the offer was made, or September 2012, using the interest rate, mortality assumptions, and loading factors used by PBGC. This method uses the survey that PBGC takes of recent prices of group annuities to derive the interest factors that are used to calculate the present value of future benefit-payment obligations under section 4044 of the Employee Retirement Income Security Act of 1974 (ERISA). These future benefits are obligations that PBGC must pay to participants in the plans that they have taken over as trustee.[8]

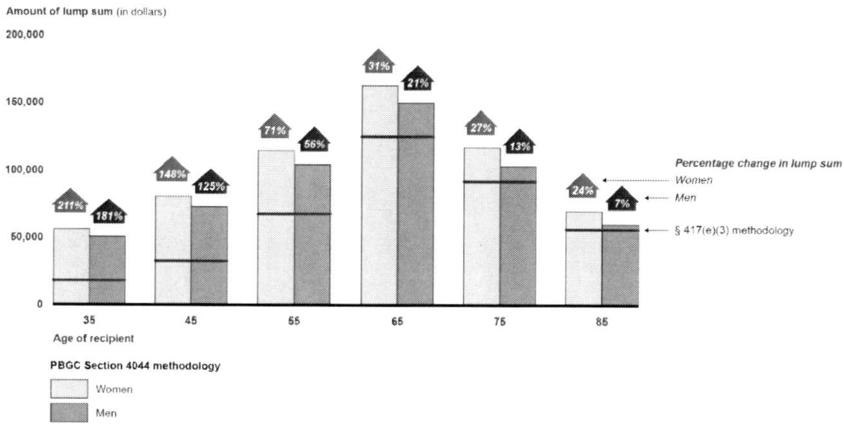

Source: GAO analysis of U.S. Department of the Treasury (Internal Revenue Service) and Pension Benefit Guaranty Corporation (PBGC) data. | GAO-15-74

Note: Analysis assumes a $10,000 annual benefit (or $833 monthly). The annuity begins at the normal retirement age of 65, for those below age 65. For those age 65 or older, the participant receives an immediate annuity and the lump sum or annuity price is calculated at the participant's current age. This figure compares lump sums determined under the minimum required methodology that we found prevalent in participant materials against lump sums that were determined using the group annuity methodology published by PBGC, applicable to the time of the offer. The statutory minimum lump sums use the August 2011 interest rates (for the 2012 plan year) of 1.85, 4.62, and 6.02 percent using the unisex mortality table prescribed under § 417(e)(3). These lump sums are compared against lump sums using the PBGC section 4044 interest rate and mortality assumptions— including a loading factor consistent with such assumptions—for September 2012.

The September 2012 interest rate is 2.95 percent for payments due within 20 years, and 3.66 for payments due beyond 20 years. We assume September 2012 rates because this is the rate in the month prior to October 2012, when we note a number of offers were made.

Figure 7. Lump Sum Payments Based on § 417(e)(3) Methodology and Sex-specific PBGC Group Annuity Methodology, with Payment Based on a $10,000 Annual Benefit Due at Age 65.

As observed earlier in the report, figure 7 shows that lump sum payments under the minimum method prescribed under § 417(e)(3) can be significantly smaller than the lump sums that would be necessary to repurchase an annuity that matches the benefit forgone under the participant's plan. In this case, and because retail annuity data is not easily available, we used a group annuity methodology consistent with PBGC section 4044 assumptions.[9] For example, a 55-year-old female would receive a lump sum payment of $67,020 under the § 417(e)(3) minimum, while she would need $114,460, or a 71 percent larger lump sum, to purchase an annuity that would have been provided under her plan (in this case, a $10,000 annual, or $833 monthly, benefit starting at age 65). As noted earlier in the report, group annuities are generally only available to large pension plans, and retail annuities are generally more expensive due to adverse selection and administrative charges or other fees, so an individual would likely need an even larger lump sum payment to replicate their prior benefit on the retail market.

Figure 8 illustrates the potential effect of excluding certain additional plan benefits from the lump sum calculation by looking at one type of additional plan benefit, subsidized early retirement—in this case, a plan with a normal retirement age of 65 but that offers unreduced early retirement at age 60. It compares the baseline lump sum that assumes retirement at age 65, versus a calculation that includes the value of the additional plan benefit by assuming the participant would have retired at age 60. This analysis assumes that the participant is eligible for, or could become eligible for, such early retirement under the plan. Figure 8 shows that only those participants who have not reached retirement age (or early retirement age) are impacted by the early retirement provision. This occurs because these participants will receive their benefits in the future. Those age 65 or older are already eligible or receiving monthly benefits under the plan at the time of their lump sum offer. A few (3) participants we interviewed noted that they believed they would qualify for early retirement under their plan, but we were unable to determine if they were indeed eligible. Formal eligibility aside, participants may find it useful to know how much their lump sum would be if the early retirement subsidy were included so they can understand the impact it might have on their lump sum offer. The differences in lump sum payments can be significant. For example, in figure 8, a 55-year-old participant would receive a $67,020 lump sum payment if the normal retirement age of 65 is assumed. However, if the plan benefits are assumed to be payable at the early retirement age of 60, the same participant would receive $101,780 —or a 52 percent larger lump sum.

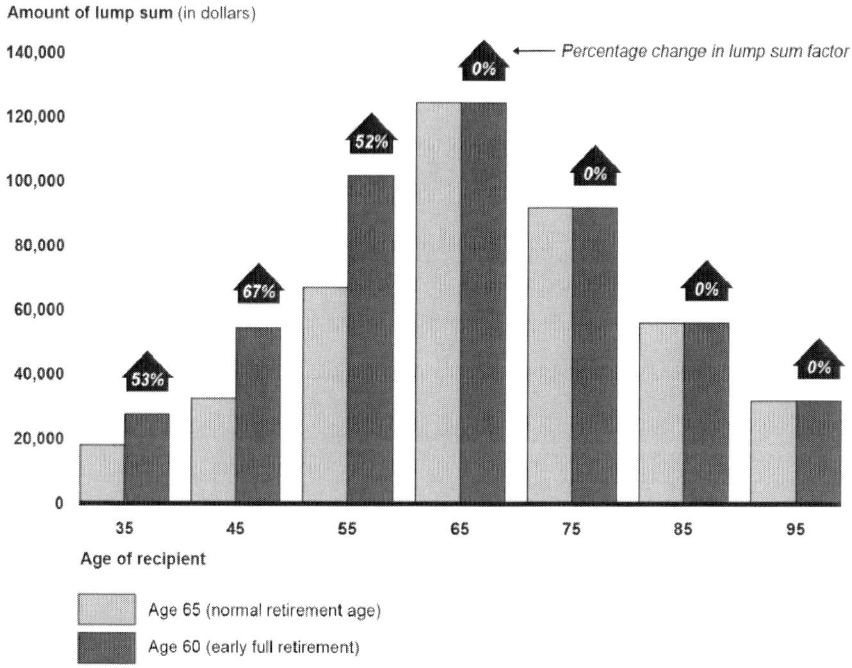

Source: GAO analysis of U.S. Department of the Treasury (Internal Revenue Service) data. | GAO-15-74

Note: Analysis assumes a $10,000 annual benefit (or $833 monthly) for both scenarios. For those offers made at or after age 65, the participant is already receiving the annuity—the annuity is assumed to be immediate and the lump sum is calculated at the participant's current age. Both scenarios assume a lump sum offer made in October 2012 using the sponsor-elected August 2011 interest rates (for the 2012 plan year). The August 2011 interest rates (for the 2012 plan year) are 1.85, 4.62, and 6.02 percent. Both scenarios use the 2012 mortality table under § 417(e)(3). One lump sum offer assumes the annuity would have been deferred until the normal retirement age of 65.

The other lump sum offer assumes the annuity would have been deferred to the plan's early retirement age, in this case age 60.

Figure 8. Lump Sum Payments Based on § 417(e)(3) Methodology Using Plan Normal Retirement Age and Early Retirement Age, by Selected Ages, with Payment Based on a $10,000 Annual Benefit Due at Age 65.

End Notes

[1] Based on 2013 Pension Benefit Guaranty Corporation premium filings for single-employer defined benefit plans.

[2] Note that all the subsequent discussion about plan sponsors is referring to private sector single-employer plan sponsors.

[3] Pub. L. No. 93-406, 88 Stat. 829.

[4] Funded status is a comparison of plan assets to plan liabilities. One measure of funded status is the "funded ratio," which is calculated by dividing plan assets by plan liabilities. Another measure of funded status is the difference between plan assets and plan liabilities, that is, the dollar amount of surplus (if plan assets exceed plan liabilities) or unfunded liability (if plan assets are less than plan liabilities).

[5] See Statement of Financial Accounting Standards 158 (subsequently codified—see generally Accounting Standards Codification (ASC) Topic 715). The 2006 accounting standard change by the Financial Accounting Standards Board (FASB) requires private sector single-employer plan sponsors to recognize the funded status of plans on their balance sheet. Under FASB's standards, plan funded status will vary with changes in asset values and interest rates. As a result, the funded status of a plan can be volatile over time, resulting in fluctuations to the plan sponsor's balance sheet.

[6] In 2011, according to DOL data, private sector employers sponsored just under 44,000 single-employer defined benefit plans, down from approximately 111,000 in 1990. Meanwhile, growth of single-employer defined contribution plans continued during the same period, with the number of defined contribution plans totaling nearly 637,000 in 2011, up from approximately 598,000 in 1990.

[7] This delineation was used by the ERISA Advisory Council in their 2013 report summarizing their examination of pension de-risking, presented on DOL's website: http://www.dol.gov/ebsa/publications/2013ACreport2.html.

[8] Sponsors are generally permitted by law to elect to make such offers to separated participants (also known as terminated vested participants). Whether sponsors are generally permitted to engage in the new practice of making such offers to retirees who have been receiving annuity benefits from the plan, however, is a more complicated determination raising additional legal and policy issues that have yet to be fully explored, Treasury officials have noted.

[9] When we refer to participants in this report, we are generally referring to either separated (terminated vested) or retired participants.

[10] For example, a retired participant may be able to switch their benefit annuity to another type of qualified joint and survivor annuity offered under the plan and, specifically for married retired participants, a qualified optional survivor annuity. The options offered will depend on the retired participant's marital status at the time of the offer.

[11] 29 U.S.C. § 1104(a)(1). ERISA imposes certain obligations on plan fiduciaries. Under ERISA, a person generally acts as a plan fiduciary when he or she (1) exercises any discretionary control or authority over plan management or any authority or control over plan assets, (2) renders investment advice for compensation respecting plan assets, or has authority or responsibility to do so, or (3) has any discretionary authority or responsibility over plan administration. 29 U.S.C. § 1002(21).

[12] DOL has the statutory authority to bring legal action against plan fiduciaries that do not comply with ERISA requirements. See 29 U.S.C. § 1132.

[13] GAO, *Private Pensions: Clarity of Required Reports and Disclosures Could Be Improved*, GAO-14-92 (Washington, D.C.: Nov 21, 2013).

[14] By law, the formal name of the council is The Advisory Council of Employee Welfare and Pension Benefit Plans.

[15] Between June 5 and November 4, 2013, the ERISA Advisory Council held four hearings. Over 20 expert witnesses provided testimony, representing, in part, DOL, PBGC, pension consulting firms, insurers, academics, advocacy groups, retiree groups, and plan sponsors.

[16] 26 U.S.C. § 6110(k)(3).

[17] 26 U.S.C. § 417(e)(3).

[18] We identified several Treasury regulations that apply to offers of lump sums paid out as part of a lump sum window. See, e.g., 26 C.F.R. § 1.417(a)(3)-1: Required explanation of qualified joint and survivor annuity and qualified preretirement survivor annuity; 26 C.F.R. § 1.417(e)-1: Restrictions and valuations of distributions from plans subject to sections 401(a)(11) and 417; 26 C.F.R. § 1.401(a)-20: Requirements of qualified joint and survivor annuity and qualified preretirement survivor annuity; 26 C.F.R. § 31.3405(c)-1: Withholding on eligible rollover distributions; 26 C.F.R. § 1.402(f)-1: Required explanation of eligible rollover distributions.

[19] Participants who accept the lump sum offer are allowed to roll over, or transfer, all or part of the lump sum amount into either an Individual Retirement Account (IRA) or another eligible employer plan.

[20] The regulation offers some flexibility as to how sponsors should convey this information. The sponsor can 1) state the lump sum amount as a percentage of the actuarial present value of the monthly annuity, 2) state the amount of the annuity that is the actuarial equivalent of the lump sum, or 3) state the actuarial present value of both the lump sum and the annuity.

[21] If the participant is married and the lump sum is greater than $5,000, written consent of the spouse is required for any form of benefit other than a joint and survivor annuity.

[22] In September 2014, PBGC announced that it intends to ask the Office of Management and Budget to approve a proposal requiring certain information about lump sum windows be reported as part of the annual premium filing starting with 2015 filings. See 79 Fed. Reg. 56,831 (Sept. 23, 2014). According to draft forms and instructions available to the public at the time the notice was published, the questions will relate to the number of persons offered lump sums under the window and the number of persons accepting the offer. The instructions will require only after-the-fact reporting (i.e., for windows that had recently closed), with a reporting lag of between 1 and 13 months.

[23] This is done using IRS Form 1099-R.

[24] Towers Watson, *Pension De-Risking Through Lump Sum Offers* (New York, N.Y.: 2013).

[25] Towers Watson, *U.S. Pension Risk Management—What Comes Next?* (New York, N.Y.: 2013).

[26] Aon Hewitt, *2014 Hot Topics in Retirement—Building a Strategic Focus* (Chicago, Ill.: 2014).

[27] We based our analysis on publically available information from a variety of sources, including information collected from PBGC, a participant advocacy group, SEC filings, corporate reports, and media reports. We verified this information to the extent possible. In October 2014, PBGC informed us, based on limited sources of information, that they were aware of at least 17 additional lump sum windows announced by sponsors during 2013 and 2014. However, we were not able to verify this information before the publication of this report.

[28] The number of participants offered lump sums by any one sponsor varied greatly, ranging from as few as 1,400 participants to as many as 90,000. For this selection of sponsors, the median number of participants receiving offers was 13,000.

[29] Aon Hewitt, *Pension Settlements Through Vested Terminated Lump Sum Windows* (Chicago, Ill.: 2013).

[30] IRS private letter rulings are not publicly associated with a specific requestor by name, but pension experts have presumed these two rulings were requested and received by Ford and General Motors. In one ruling (PLR 201228051), the IRS stated that a 30- to 60- day lump sum window period for participants receiving annuity benefits would not violate the minimum distribution requirements. In another ruling (PLR 201228045), the IRS stated that those requirements would not be violated by a 60- to 90- day window period. Both rulings also made clear that, except for the particular rulings specified, no opinion was expressed as to the federal tax consequences of these practices under any other provision of the Internal Revenue Code, including a number of specified Code sections, or as to the qualification of the plans at issue.

[31] Specifically, once a participant begins receiving lifetime annuity payments, those payments must not increase and the payment period may not be modified except in specific circumstances, such as due to a plan amendment providing for the payment of increased benefits. 26 U.S.C. § 401(a)(9) and 26 C.F.R. § 1.401(a)(9)-6, Q&A-14(a)(4).

[32] Experts point out that these rulings were notable to the extent they allowed plan sponsors to perform risk transfers in a manner that had not previously been explored. During 2014, six additional sponsors requested and received similar IRS private letter rulings regarding offers of lump sums to retirees in payment status, although these private letter rulings contained several caveats to the effect that their scope was limited to specified issues and did not address compliance with other plan qualification requirements or with ERISA. As with other private letter rulings, the identity of the sponsors making these additional requests was not publicly disclosed by IRS. While IRS private letter rulings interpret and apply tax laws to the requestors' represented set of facts specific to their case, the rulings may not be relied on as precedent for future cases, regardless of similarity. See 26 U.S.C. § 6110(k)(3). Thus, other sponsors considering similar actions must request their own rulings in order to ensure compliance with the Internal Revenue Code.

[33] Pub. L. No. 109-280, § 302, 120 Stat. 780, 920.

[34] Present value calculations reflect the time value of money, based on the assumption that a dollar in the future is worth less than a dollar today because the dollar today can be invested and earn interest. Using a higher interest rate will lower the present value of a stream of future payments, in this case, the lump sum amount, because it implies that a lower level of assets today would be able to fund those future payments.

[35] The extent to which lump sum amounts are lower because of the switch from 30-year Treasury rates to corporate bond rates is dependent on the age of the participant. This is because the corporate bond rates vary with how many years into the future the projected pension payments would be made. Under most economic conditions, lump sums for younger

participants would be reduced the most, and lump sums for older participants may sometimes be increased.

[36] PPA established a five-year phase-in of the switch from the 30-year Treasury bond rate to corporate bond rates for calculating lump sums. Treasury rates were still to be used for lump sum distributions in 2007, followed by weighted averages of Treasury and corporate rates for distributions in 2008 to 2011, with corporate rates being given 20 percent weight in 2008, 40 percent in 2009, 60 percent in 2010, and 80 percent in 2011, before being fully phased in for 2012 and later years.

[37] Pub. L. No. 112-141, § 40211, 126 Stat. 405, 846.

[38] Under Section 103 of PPA, lump sum payments are restricted for plans with a reported funded status below 80 percent. MAP-21 has temporarily changed the measurement of a plan's funded status for this purpose by basing the discount rate used to measure plan liabilities on a 25-year historical average of corporate bond rates rather than the 2-year average otherwise established under PPA. Specifically, MAP-21 temporarily applies what is known as an "interest rate corridor" based on the 25-year historical average. The use of a 25-year historical average has the effect of increasing discount rates, and thereby lowering the measure of plan liabilities and improving funded status, because interest rates were higher earlier in the 25-year historical period. The Highway and Transportation Funding Act of 2014 generally extended these interest rate "smoothing" provisions. Pub. L. No. 113-159, § 2003, 128 Stat. 1839, 1849.

[39] SOA released its new tables on October 27, 2014. Based on historical precedent, experts anticipate that IRS will adopt the final SOA tables for use in the calculation of lump sums, in some manner, after considering certain technical adjustments. SOA has stated that an important motivation for its study was the requirement that Treasury review prescribed mortality tables at least every 10 years. SOA also recommends that the mortality improvement model be reviewed at least every three years, and designed its model to facilitate ease of updating.

[40] In this report, we use the term "mortality tables" to refer to a combination of a base mortality table, which measures mortality rates as of a base year, and a mortality improvement projections scale, which estimates annual improvements in mortality beyond the base year. The mortality tables currently required by IRS are the RP-2000 tables with Scale AA mortality improvement. These tables form the basis for the unisex tables constructed for minimum lump sums under 26 U.S.C. § 417(e)(3). The new table released by SOA is known as RP-2014 and the mortality improvement scale is MP-2014.

[41] Specifically, the tables reflect a 10.4 percent increase in life expectancy for males age 65, with an average life expectancy of 21.6 years, up from 19.6 years. The tables reflect an 11.3 percent increase for females age 65, with an average life expectancy of 23.8 years, up from 21.4 years. The percentage increase in any lump sum will generally be somewhat less than the percentage increase in life expectancy because projected future payments are discounted with interest to determine their present value in calculating the lump sum. Also, unisex mortality tables are used for the purpose of determining optional forms of benefits from qualified pension plans, so the new mortality tables ultimately adopted by IRS will reflect some blend of male and female life expectancy.

[42] The Society of Actuaries report presents a range of calculations of single-sum annuity values, which are equivalent to lump sum calculations, under a variety of interest rate assumptions. Under one of these calculations, based on SOA's projection of required segment interest rates, SOA estimates indicate that switching to the new mortality tables in 2016 would increase hypothetical sex-specific lump sums by anywhere from 3.6 percent to 16.9 percent

for males and by 5.8 percent to 11.8 percent for females, depending on current age. These calculations assumed a pension starting age of 62 for those younger than age 62, and are shown for every tenth age from ages 25 through 85. The impact is lowest at age 55 for males and age 65 for females, and is greater at younger and older ages. Actual lump sums are based on unisex tables, so estimated increases would be somewhere in between these sex-distinct estimates. Also, as already noted, there are technical choices that the IRS would have to make in adopting these tables, and one of these is whether projections of future mortality improvement should be "static" (where the degree of mortality improvement varies only by age) or "generational" (where the improvement varies by both age and calendar year). The current IRS methodology for determining minimum lump sums uses the static approach, but SOA recommends using the generational approach for pension measurements, and the estimates of lump sum increases presented here assume that the IRS adopts the generational approach.

[43] PBGC premium rate increases were included in section 40211 of MAP-21 in 2012, and in the Bipartisan Budget Act of 2013. Pub. L. No. 113-67, § 703, 127 Stat. 1165, 1190-92. This is also a potential incentive to conduct a group annuity buy-out.

[44] Rates will be indexed for inflation beyond 2016.

[45] This reduction of premium costs will continue to accrue to the sponsor for each additional year that the removed participant would have otherwise been in the plan.

[46] This can be partly due to the fact that this group will generally consist of younger participants compared to the group of participants already in pay status. As a result, these participants' accrued benefits will be discounted for a greater length of time due to their younger ages.

[47] Russell Research, *Update: Risk transfer options for defined benefit plan sponsors* (East Rutherford, N.J., 2013).

[48] Specifically, a sponsor may elect a stability period of up to one year combined with a maximum lookback of up to 5 months. This means that the interest rates used at the time of the offer may be nearly 17 months old relative to rates that are current just before the offer.

[49] IRS officials said that the ability to selectively choose a "lookback" month is constrained in the case of a plan that already has a lump sum benefit—even if the lump sum distributions are less than $5,000 and are paid without employee consent. This is because a plan can have only one provision for "lookback."

[50] Specifically, IRS officials explained that the "lookback" rule was created to help with the administration of plans that offer lump sums as an ongoing optional form of benefit. When applied to those types of lump sums, sponsors lock in a single "lookback" rate to be used for all lump sums calculated during a specified period, such as a plan year. Due to interest rate fluctuations over the course of that period, the "lookback" rate may favor the plan sponsor at certain times and the plan participant at other times. However, in the case of a one-time lump sum window, the IRS officials said sponsors, in essence, have perfect hindsight and will select "lookback" rates that will minimize the overall amount of lump sum payments on the specified calculation date.

[51] In defined benefit plans, early retirement benefits are often actuarially reduced to reflect the fact that someone retiring at an early retirement age will collect benefits sooner, and for a longer period of time, than someone retiring at normal retirement age. A subsidized early retirement benefit is one in which the early retirement benefit is reduced by less than a full actuarial reduction; one example of such a benefit would be an unreduced early retirement benefit. Similarly, a subsidized joint-and-survivor annuity is one in which the reduction to the plan's single life annuity benefit is less than the full actuarial reduction that would account for the fact that a joint-and-survivor annuity is paid out, on average, for a longer

period of time than a single life annuity. Lastly, an example of a supplemental early retirement benefit would be a temporary additional benefit paid from an early retirement age to normal retirement age.

[52] It is important to note that this incentive, unlike the other incentives we examined, will only apply to plans that have provisions for certain additional plan benefits for separated former participants. Additional plan benefits, such as subsidized early retirement benefits, are more commonly offered to plan participants who are still employees of the plan sponsor and retire from the plan sponsor, but they are sometimes offered to separated former participants as well.

[53] PLR 201228045.

[54] Note that reducing the size of the plan relative to the size of the plan sponsor, and removing pension liabilities for participants who had never worked for the plan sponsor, may also serve as incentives to conduct a group annuity buy-out.

[55] Note that some of these considerations—sizable immediate payments, interest rate uncertainty, foregone potential returns, and to a lesser extent, administrative costs—may also serve as disincentives to conduct a group annuity buy-out.

[56] The method sponsors must use for determining the minimum lump sum value of an annuity benefit is statutorily prescribed in 26 U.S.C. § 417(e)(3).

[57] These reductions in retirement income can also be thought of as the gap between the amount of lump sum offered and the amount of lump sum that would be needed to replicate the pension benefit.

[58] Note that since figure 1 is based on a group annuity methodology and does not correct for the differences in pricing between the group annuity and the retail annuity market, it thus understates the potential reduction in retirement income from accepting a lump sum window offer and using the lump sum to purchase a replacement annuity. A group annuity is a type of annuity that is generally available to purchasers of annuities for a collection of individuals, such as a group of participants in a pension plan, and where there is no option to opt out of the annuity. For example, a large pension plan that purchases annuities for its participants as part of a plan termination may purchase a group annuity contract for the participants under the plan. See appendix II for more discussion of the methodology used in figure 1.

[59] See GAO, *Pension Plan Valuation: Views on Using Multiple Measures to Offer a More Complete Financial Picture,* GAO-14-264 (Washington, D.C.: September 30, 2014).

[60] As of the date underlying the data in figure 1, the discount rates for determining minimum required lump sums were 1.85 percent for projected pension payments that would have been due in less than 5 years, 4.62 percent for payments that would have been due in 5 to 20 years, and 6.02 percent for payments of more than 20 years. In contrast, the discount rates underlying the estimated group annuity rates were 2.95 percent for payments that would have been due within 20 years, and 3.66 for payments that would have been due beyond 20 years. See appendix II for more detail.

[61] Assuming that men and women of equivalent ages have a common life expectancy is known as unisex, or gender neutral, life expectancy. Specifically, for lump sum distributions that are subject to 26 U.S.C. § 417(e), a unisex mortality table is used to determine the minimum lump sum, and lump sum rates must be the same for men and women even if lump sum rates in excess of the minimum are used.

62 A group annuity is a type of annuity that has generally favorable pricing and low administrative costs because the insurer is able to spread longevity risk across a large population of individuals. These types of group annuities are available to large purchasers

of annuities for a group of individuals, for example, large pension plans. Most former participants are unlikely to have an available retirement vehicle that will allow them access to a group annuity with their lump sum.

[63] This advice is consistent with other expert observations. For example, the American Academy of Actuaries notes that defined benefit plans tend to be a more cost effective source of annuities than outside a defined benefit plan because of savings in administrative costs and the absence of profit margins, among other reasons.

[64] Some participants may also be allowed to roll over their lump sum into a tax-qualified defined contribution plan, such as a 401(k) plan. However, we focus on IRA rollovers as they appear to be most prevalent and the risks and characteristics of such plans are in many ways similar.

[65] GAO has reviewed a particular type of annuity product that has guaranteed lifetime withdrawal features that can help older Americans ensure that they do not outlive their assets. Consumers can potentially benefit from these products by having a steady stream of income regardless of how their investment assets perform or how long they live, while at the same time maintaining access to their assets for unexpected or other expenses. However, these products are complex and present some risks to consumers, and require them to make multiple important decisions similar to those participants face during the spend-down phase of a lump sum. See GAO, *Retirement Security: Annuities with Guaranteed Lifetime Withdrawals Have Both Benefits and Risks, but Regulation Varies across States*, GAO-13-75 (Washington, D.C.: Dec. 10, 2012).

[66] GAO, *401(k) Plans: Labor and IRS Could Improve the Rollover Process for Participants*, GAO-13-30 (Washington, D.C.: March 7, 2013).

[67] U.S. Library of Congress, CRS, *Converting Retirement Savings into Income: Annuities and Periodic Withdrawals*, by Janemarie Mulvey and Patrick Purcell, CRS Report R40008 (Washington, DC: Office of Congressional Information and Publishing, Feb. 2, 2009).

[68] Note that figure 2 assumes regular, periodic withdrawals in the spend-down of the lump sum.

[69] See L. Frolik, *Rethinking ERISA's Promise of Income Security in a World of 401(k) Plans*, (University of Pittsburgh School of Law: March 2013). In addition, diminished capacity that impacts general financial decision-making may make older adults particularly susceptible to financial exploitation. See GAO, *Elder Justice: National Strategy Needed to Effectively Combat Elder Financial Exploitation*, GAO-13-110 (Washington, D.C.: November 15, 2012).

[70] GAO-13-30.

[71] The specific investment products held in 401(k) plans and IRAs, as well as the various financial professionals who service them, are subject to oversight from applicable securities, banking, or insurance regulators, which can include both federal and state regulators. For example, mutual funds, offered in both plans and IRAs, are generally regulated by the Securities and Exchange Commission (SEC), which requires funds to disclose fees and to inform investors of products' potential risks. An investment adviser provides a wide range of investment advisory services, including management of client portfolios. Investment advisers manage the portfolios of individuals as well as the portfolios of pension funds and mutual funds. Broker-dealers provide brokerage services where they act as an agent for someone else; a dealer acts as a principal for its own account. SEC has primary responsibility for oversight of investment advisers and broker-dealers, while those who sell insurance products are also subject to state insurance regulation. Investment advisers, broker-dealers, and insurance agents are subject to different standards of practice.

[72] Witnesses at the 2013 ERISA Advisory Council hearings on Private Sector Pension De-risking and Participant Protections noted that the elderly may be particularly "vulnerable to pressure from relatives or investment advisors, and, in some cases, diminished in their capacity to weigh the pros and cons of the options" with respect to a lump sum election.

[73] GAO-13-30.

[74] See Aon Hewitt, *Pension Settlements Through Terminated Vested Lump Sum Windows: Insights into Plan Sponsor Experience*, February 2013. The observation that just over half of participants elect to roll over their lump sum is consistent with our interviews of participants. Among the participants we interviewed, 15 out of 37 accepted the lump sum window offer. Of those that accepted, 13 said they rolled over most of their monies into an IRA.

[75] Ibid. The study also notes that the direct rollover rate increased with the size of the lump sum, which suggests that the dollar-weighted value of direct rollovers is larger than 51 percent. A direct rollover is when a participant specifies the plan or IRA to which their distribution should be transferred. The plan can transfer the money via a non-transferable check made out to the receiving entity or electronically. Indirect rollovers are another option for maintaining the lump sum in the qualified retirement system, but the study notes that many participants that cash out their lump sum do not rollover the monies at a later date, resulting in a leakage of funds out of the retirement system. Indirect rollovers are rollovers wherein the participant's plan writes a check payable to the participant for some or all of the lump sum. The participant then disburses those funds within 60 days of receipt of the check to a qualified plan that will accept the monies or to an IRA. Our IRA rollover report, GAO-13-30, also discusses the different types of rollovers.

[76] In some cases, leakage might not be a retirement security problem. For example, an individual who has adequate other sources of retirement income may be able to afford to use a pension lump sum for other purposes, such as a bequest.

[77] U.S. Social Security Administration, Office of Policy, *Perspectives: Does Retirement Education Teach People to Save Pension Distributions?* by Leslie A. Muller Social Security Bulletin, Vol. 64 No. 4 (2001/2002).

[78] In some cases, taking a lump sum to use for these other purposes could be the most appropriate decision given the participant's particular circumstances. This assessment involves broader and more complex issues of poverty or insufficient overall wealth or income, which are beyond the scope of this report.

[79] As described more fully in the background section of this report, sponsors are required to provide participants some of the information GAO determined was key to participants' decisions as to whether to elect a lump sum.

[80] Most of the materials we analyzed were provided to us by participants who had received them rather than by plan sponsors. As such, we cannot be certain that the materials we reviewed were accurate and complete representations of the materials provided by plan sponsors to participants. Further, our limited review of these materials did not constitute a compliance review, so while we observed that sponsors appeared to provide certain required materials, we did not assess the adequacy of those materials or reach any determinations as to whether such materials complied with any applicable legal requirements.

[81] An immediate annuity is an annuity for which the participant is eligible at his or her current age. A deferred annuity is one for which the participant will be eligible at a later age, such as 65 for normal retirement, or, for example, age 60 for early retirement.

[82] For a detailed explanation of how we assessed for our factors when reviewing packets, please see appendix I, table 3.

[83] Defined benefit plan sponsors are required to provide a pension benefit statement to all plan participants at least once every 3 years. In addition, defined benefit plan participants may annually request a benefit statement.

[84] According to participants we interviewed, the materials the plan sponsor provided compared the value of the annuity at age 65 to the value of the lump sum and did not make clear that unreduced benefits were available at age 60.

[85] Six packets provided the interest rates used to develop the relative value notice, but no mention was made regarding whether these rates were also used in calculating the lump sum. GAO did not consider the inclusion of these interest rates sufficient for participants' purposes in assessing the lump sum offer.

[86] Some (12 of 33) participants assumed that their lump sum payment had been calculated based on a single life expectancy and wished that their plan sponsor had told them this figure explicitly. In actuality, lump sum calculations are not based upon a single life expectancy figure, but upon a set of mortality probabilities for different ages provided in a mortality table. However, only one packet we reviewed demonstrated how mortality assumptions were incorporated into the lump sum calculation.

[87] 26 C.F.R. § 1.417(a)(3)-1(c)(1)(iv) and (v). In its bulletin accompanying the issuance of the final regulations on the Relative Value Notice (Internal Revenue Bulletin 2006-16), IRS states that the regulations were developed to help plan participants compare different forms of their pension benefits "without professional advice." The regulation offers some flexibility as to how sponsors should convey this information. Specifically, the sponsor can 1) state the lump sum amount as a percentage of the actuarial present value of the monthly annuity, 2) state the amount of the annuity that is the actuarial equivalent of the lump sum, or 3) state the actuarial present value of both the lump sum and the annuity.

[88] As noted earlier, the value of the lump sum payment may be substantially lower than what it would cost to purchase a retail annuity.

[89] In addition to the relative value notice, IRS, in a notice of proposed rulemaking published in 2008, noted that PPA instructed the Secretary of the Treasury "to provide that the description of a participant's right, if any, to defer receipt of a distribution shall also describe the consequences of failing to defer such receipt." Notice to Participants of Consequences of Failing to Defer Receipt of Qualified Retirement Plan Distributions; Expansion of Applicable Election Period and Period for Notices, 73 Fed. Reg. 59,575 (to be codified at 26 C.F.R. pt. 1) (Oct. 9, 2008). To that end, the proposed regulations would have required that, in the case of a defined benefit plan, the participant be provided a description of the specified federal tax implications of failing to defer, as well as a statement of the amount payable to the participant under the normal form of benefit both upon immediate commencement and as a deferred annuity benefit (at the later of age 62 or attainment of normal retirement age). The proposed regulation would also have increased the length of lump sum election period to 180 days. The proposed rule has not been finalized.

[90] Under the minimum required lump sum calculation under 26 U.S.C. § 417(e)(3), the present value of benefits is generally calculated at the plan-specified normal retirement age. Such calculation might not include certain additional plan benefits, such as early retirement subsidies. (For more details about how the treatment of certain additional plan benefits affects the lump sum payment, see appendix II.)

[91] Specifically, because the participant would not be eligible for the additional plan benefits under either the lump sum or immediate annuity options, this comparison might show the two options to have "approximately the same value" without disclosing that the value of the deferred annuity option would be higher than either of those options.

[92] While some (12) participants told us they performed more advanced calculations that adjusted for the time value of money, others (12) told us they did not.

[93] On June 26, 2013, the Supreme Court of the United States ruled, in *United States v. Windsor*, that section 3 of the Defense of Marriage Act (DOMA) is unconstitutional. 570 U.S. ____,133 S. Ct. 2675 (2013). Section 3 provides that, in any federal statute, the term "marriage" means a legal union between one man and one woman as husband and wife, and that "spouse" refers only to a person of the opposite sex who is a husband or wife. Subsequently, on September 18, 2013, the Department of Labor released guidance indicating that ERISA and DOL's ERISA regulations would be read as recognizing all legal marriages of same-sex couples regardless of where the couple lived. See: Technical Release No. 2013-04: Guidance to Employee Benefit Plans on the Definition of "Spouse" and "Marriage" under ERISA and the Supreme Court's Decision in United States v. Windsor.

[94] As demonstrated by research from the field of behavioral finance and economics, emotion and intuition can play a role in financial decision-making, as people are not always rational as would be assumed under conventional financial and economic theory.

[95] In 2009, IRS issued Internal Revenue Bulletin 200-39, Notice 2009-68, which contains safe harbor explanations and model notices for plans offering rollover distributions, which would occur, for example, under a lump sum window. The model notice provides, among other items, a discussion of 1) how a rollover may affect a participant's tax situation, 2) additional income taxes from early distributions, and 3) state income taxes. While we did not assess sponsor compliance, we observed in our review of sponsor materials that the included tax materials often appeared to be very similar to the model notice.

[96] Technically, pension payments are paid out of the plan, not by the plan sponsor. The sponsor's obligation is to make required, actuarially determined contributions to the plan. So a plan sponsor cannot "default on its promise to pay pension benefits," but can default on its required contributions to the plan.

[97] While PBGC faces some long-term financial challenges, we found that many participants were not well informed about the agency and the level of benefit protection it could afford them. According to a 2008 PBGC report, approximately 84 percent of participants from sampled defined benefit plans had vested benefits that would be fully guaranteed by PBGC. PBGC trusteed the 125 sampled plans on which the analysis was based from 1990 to 2005. See PBGC, *PBGC Guarantee Limits—An Update* (Washington, D.C.: September 2008). For information on long-term PBGC financial challenges identified by GAO, see: GAO, *High Risk Series: An Update,* GAO-13-283 (Washington, D.C.: February 2013), 46-48.

[98] Many of these participants (6 of 10) cited both of these concerns.

End Note for Appendix I

[1] As noted previously, we did not reach any determinations as to whether individual sponsors complied with the applicable federal requirements. Instead, we focused on whether the materials provided by sponsors to participants satisfied the eight factors we had identified as key to informed participant decision-making.

End Notes for Appendix II

[1] This inverse relationship occurs because present value calculations reflect the time value of money. A dollar in the future is worth less than a dollar today, because the dollar today can be invested and earn interest. Using a higher interest rate will lower the present value of a stream of payments—or, in this case the lump sum—because it implies that a lower level of assets will be needed to fund those future payments.

[2] In the case of a retired participant, the participant would already be receiving monthly benefits, so the lump sum would be the present value of projected remaining benefit payments under the plan. In the case of a terminated vested participant, the participant is entitled to a deferred annuity, that is, payments are due to commence at some date in the future. This contrasts with an immediate annuity in which the participant is about to begin receiving benefits with no deferral period.

[3] Mortality tables are often constructed using a snapshot of age-specific mortality rates based on study of experience from the recent past, and are often used in combination with a table to project future mortality improvement.

[4] For ease of reference, we refer to this simply as § 417(e)(3) throughout this appendix.

[5] A yield curve is a graph that shows interest rates of bonds of common credit quality at a set point in time plotted on the vertical axis, and time, known as the maturity date, plotted on the horizontal axis. A common yield curve compares U.S. Treasury securities of various maturities. Long-term rates usually are higher than short-term rates because the risks posed by inflation and the possible default of the borrower rise with the length of time over which credit is extended. Therefore, most of the time, the yield curve slopes upward from left to right.

[6] In addition, a PBGC official said, as an additional check, the calculations were validated using a separate calculator made by a PBGC contractor.

[7] Figure 6 specifically uses 2012 unisex mortality tables using the MP-2014 projection scale—with mortality improvement applied generationally—for the alternative calculation. To construct a 2012 unisex mortality table from the RP-2014 mortality tables and mortality improvement scales from the Society of Actuaries' (SOA) RPEC, we backcasted the employee and healthy annuitant tables for males and females by the mortality improvement recommended by SOA (mortality improvement scale MP-2014). We then created a combined table from the separate employee and healthy annuitant tables for each gender, using the implied ratios in the 2012 § 417(e)(3) table. Technically, these are sex-specific tables used for § 430(h), but since the unisex tables under § 417(e)(3) are simply an average of the combined, sex-specific tables under § 430(h), we created a 2012 unisex table accordingly. To incorporate generational mortality improvement, which means that we project each age cohort to experience the projected probability of mortality in each future year, we adjusted for projected improvement within each calendar year that the individual ages. (For example, a 35-year-old would have the probability of death of a 35- year-old in 2012, the probability of death (adjusted for any improvement) of a 36-year-old in 2013, and so on, until the individual has a certain probability of death at age 120 in the year 2097).

[8] The PBGC methodology uses a mortality table with similarities to the § 417(e)(3) table except that gender-specific tables are used.

[9] Additionally, a loading factor consistent with 4044 assumptions is added to the lump sum. In the case of the annuity prices, which are all less than $200,000, this is a charge of 5 percent of the preliminary annuity price plus $200. For a more detailed description of loading assumptions for all annuity prices, see Appendix C to 29 C.F.R. Part 4044.

In: Private Pensions, Lump Sum Offer... ISBN: 978-1-63483-263-2
Editor: James G. Hughes

Chapter 2

PRIVATE SECTOR PENSION DE-RISKING AND PARTICIPANT PROTECTIONS*

Advisory Council on Employee Welfare and Pension Benefit Plans

ABSTRACT

The 2013 ERISA Advisory Council examined the increased level of activity by defined benefit pension plan sponsors to reduce their risks in order to assess the potential need for further guidance, clarification, and potential educational opportunities by the Department. The Council acknowledged from the outset the important distinction between settlor and fiduciary functions involved in the making and implementation of such plan decisions. The Council sought to identify particular concerns relating to current de-risking strategies that might warrant further guidance, clarification, or education, with particular emphasis on the impact that these strategies might have on participants and their retirement security.

Based upon the testimony received during three days of hearings, the Council is presenting recommendations in the following areas:

- confirmation of the scope of Interpretive Bulletin (IB) 95-1, and possible creation of one or more safe harbors;

* This is an edited, reformatted and augmented version of report to the Honorable Thomas E. Perez, United States Secretary of Labor, issued November 2013.

- participant disclosures;
- interpretive guidance on the scope of ERISA Section 502(a)(9);
- education and outreach to plan sponsors on issues surrounding volatility in pension plans; and
- collection of information on de-risking transactions.

I. EXECUTIVE SUMMARY

The Council heard testimony that confirmed recent increases in defined benefit plan de-risking activity. Recent de-risking activity might be more appropriately referred to as risk transfer, because removal of risk from the plan sponsor often results in a corresponding increase in risk for another party. Those parties are generally either an insurer (in the event of an annuity purchase) or the participant (in the event of a lump sum payment, in which case responsibilities and risks associated with investing and managing the lump sum and satisfaction of retirement income needs fall to the participant). The reasons for this increase in activity may be attributable to several factors ranging from (i) changes to funding rules and accounting standards which cause plan funding volatility and impact on financial statements, respectively; (ii) changes in the interest rates used for calculation of lump sum distributions; and (iii) a general disconnect between the defined benefit plan itself and the employer's current view of its mission.

The Council received written and/or in-person testimony from twenty-two witnesses across a broad spectrum of interested parties, including governmental representatives of the Employee Benefit Security Administration (EBSA) of DOL, the Pension Benefit Guaranty Corporation, and the District of Columbia Department of Insurance, Securities and Banking (DISB), as well as the National Organization of Life and Health Guaranty Associations (NOLHGA), and also representatives from the employee, employer, consultant/actuarial, legal, and insurance communities.

Issues discussed over the course of three days of hearings included:

- Identifying significant factors contributing to the increase in de-risking activity, and ascertaining whether one or more of such factors give rise to the need for regulatory modifications or clarifications, or additional education.
- Distinguishing between the separate roles of settlor and fiduciary, which may be performed by different individuals or by the same

person(s), and identifying where those roles might overlap, create conflicts, or give rise to the need for additional disclosure or safeguards.

- Exploring specific de-risking alternatives, including plan provisions for lump sum distributions, annuity purchases, and other alternatives.
- Analyzing the need for participant protections across the range of potential de-risking alternatives.

Based upon the testimony received during three days of hearings, the Council is presenting recommendations in the following areas:

- confirmation of the scope of IB 95-1;
- participant disclosures;
- interpretive guidance on the scope of ERISA Section 502(a)(9);
- education and outreach to plan sponsors on issues surrounding volatility in pension plans; and
- collection of information on de-risking transactions.

II. RECOMMENDATIONS

A. The Council recommends that DOL confirm that IB 95-1 applies to any purchase of an annuity from an insurer as a distribution of benefits under a defined benefit plan, not just purchases coincident with a plan termination. The Council also recommends that DOL consider the development of safe harbors within the scope of the Interpretive Bulletin for such purchases. Such safe harbor(s) could include two or more factors drawn from IB 95-1 and/or the following:

1. Procedural safeguards by the plan sponsor, the insurer, or both, with respect to resolving disputes regarding the benefits to be paid to a former plan participant under the annuity;
2. Contractual provisions, to the extent practicable, which replicate one or more protections that employees receive under ERISA and which are otherwise consistent with the terms of the contract;
3. Requirements for notices and valuation procedures similar to those required for lump sum distributions, if offered under the plan; and/or
4. The anti-alienation provisions of Part 2, Title 1 of ERISA.

B. The Council recommends that DOL require that a defined benefit pension plan providing participants with an option of a lump sum distribution within a specified window, with or without a separate option of the distribution of an annuity described in IB 95-1:

1. Provide similar disclosures to participants, at least 90 days prior to the action to be taken, as would be required under current PBGC termination regulations (29 C.F.R. §§ 4041.23, 24 & 27); and
2. Include in such disclosures relevant information to enable the participant to make an informed election, including where applicable:
   a) the potential impact of tax penalties on any past annuity distributions;
   b) whether an early retirement or other subsidy is included in the calculation of the lump sum distribution; and
   c) an equivalent comparison of a lump sum distribution to the benefit otherwise payable under the plan or under a purchased annuity contract.

C. The Council recommends that DOL consider providing guidance under ERISA Section 502(a)(9) to provide clarity to plan fiduciaries regarding the consequences of a breach of fiduciary duty in the selection of an annuity contract for distribution out of the plan, including guidance for the term "appropriate relief" (e.g., whether monetary relief is available) and under what circumstances "posting of security" generally may be necessary.

D. The Council recommends that DOL provide education and outreach to plan sponsors:

1) On the range of options available for de-risking, including asset-liability matching (also referred to as "liability driven investing," or LDI), purchases and holding of annuities under the plan ("buy-ins"), hedging, lump sum distributions and distributions of annuities from the plan ("buy-outs");
2) On the distinction between settlor and fiduciary functions in de-risking transactions; and
3) On the distinctions between disclosure, education, and advice in assisting participants in making elections of buy-outs in light of current and future guidance from the Department.

E. The Council recommends that DOL consider the potential benefits of collecting relevant information regarding plan de-risking in the form of lump sum windows and annuity purchases outside the context of a plan termination. Such information might include such factors as:

1) Length of lump sum window;
2) Whether the lump sum window was an alternative to an annuity purchase (i.e., an annuity purchase if lump sum not elected);
3) Number and/or percent of relevant cohorts (e.g., term vested participants, retirees in pay status, union participants, etc.);
4) Number and/or percent of eligible participants who elected the lump sum;
5) Number and/or percent of participants who elected the lump sum and elected a direct rollover to another plan or IRA;
6) Dollar value of lump sums and annuity purchases and percent of the assets before and after the transaction(s); and
7) Name of insurance carrier(s) issuing the annuity contracts and/or certificates.

III. BACKGROUND

There has been an increased level of activity by sponsors of single-employer defined benefit pension plans to terminate the plans in their entirety, or purchase annuities and/or offer lump sum distributions to some or all of their plan participants. These participants can include both former employees with vested deferred benefits and retirees currently receiving pension distributions from the plan in the form of an annuity.

This activity is sometimes referred to generally as "de-risking" or "risk transfer." One of the purposes of risk transfer is to reduce or eliminate the plan sponsor's risk for their current and future liabilities. However, by so doing, it also transfers the risks associated with current or future pension obligations to another party, which is either the participant (in the form of a lump sum), an insurance company (in the form of a distributed annuity), or both.

Commentators have proffered many reasons for this trend in de-risking ranging from plan sponsors' desires to reduce the impact of the volatility of their pension plan obligations on their financial statements and in their funding requirements; the revised mortality and interest rates in the Pension Protection Act and subsequent legislation providing for pension funding relief; the current interest rate environment; the desire to lower administrative costs, including reduction or elimination of rising PBGC premiums; the current and future funding status of the plan; and/or considerations unique to a specific plan sponsor or industry. And, they have noted, in the case of annuity purchases, the guarantees of the contract issuer as well as state guaranty fund coverage.

Other commentators have voiced concerns for participants ranging from participants' lack of understanding about the benefits of lifetime income streams; challenges for individuals in investing effectively or in adequately addressing longevity risk; the adequacy, scope and independence of education, counseling, and/or investment advice to participants as to whether they should take the lump sum and where they should invest their distributions; the potential for adverse tax consequences for current retirees who receive a lump sum after commencing retirement distributions; absence of fiduciary and PBGC protections following distributions or annuity purchases; the capacity of insurance companies to support a substantial growth in demand for annuities; the capacity of state insurance guaranty associations to backstop insurance company guarantees to a similar level as current PBGC protections; and potential impacts on employee retirement security and adequacy.

Many plan design decisions (including a decision to offer partial or full lump sums as well as a decision to establish, maintain or terminate a plan) are generally settlor functions which do not give rise to fiduciary responsibilities in and of themselves. Nevertheless, most of the specific actions taken to implement such decisions involve important fiduciary considerations and may significantly impact plan participants.

The Council's examination focused on the following:

A. What are the reasons plan sponsors are choosing to transfer risk? Are there common developments or factors that lead to this decision? Are the reasons more likely to be specific to the circumstances and considerations of the individual plan sponsor? What are the advantages and disadvantages to the plan and plan sponsor? What types of plans and plan sponsors, by size, industry, etc. have adopted "risk-transfer" activities? Is the incidence of plan terminations, plan distributions of annuities, and/or addition or modification of lump sum features in private sector defined benefit plans increasing or is it likely to increase when interest rates rise and/or funding improves?
B. Employers who have adopted de-risking strategies have offered various combinations of lump sum distributions and annuities to

subsets of their plan populations. Some employers have chosen to terminate the plan entirely. What are the different alternatives for plans and plan sponsors? Why do they choose these alternatives? What are the factors or criteria used for choosing these alternatives? If plan sponsors do not terminate the entire plan, what is the impact, if any, on the plan and the remaining participants?

C. What are the current requirements and limitations, if any, on the ability of a private employer defined benefit plan sponsor to: (1) add, modify or remove a lump sum (or partial lump sum) option for one or more groups of plan participants, (2) terminate the plan, or (3) distribute annuities for all or a subset of plan participants (including but not limited to the selection of the annuity provider under IB 95-1)? Should DOL consider updates or revisions to any of these rules, requirements, or limitations?

D. Are there unique issues involved in decisions on risk-transfer being made by ERISA plan fiduciaries that also perform settlor functions? Is guidance needed on these issues?

E. What are the interests of plan participants in determining whether to accept a lump sum in lieu of retaining a benefit under the plan? What are the advantages and disadvantages to plan participants? Are there patterns of acceptance or rejection of lump sum options, across specific demographics or account sizes, which may be relevant to the Department in reviewing its rules and requirements?

F. What are the current participant disclosure requirements applicable to each potential change to the plan? Do participants have sufficient information to make an informed choice? Do these requirements adequately protect the interests of plan participants? If not, should there be checklists, model disclosures, or other proposals, which would protect the interests of plan participants while recognizing that plan design, amendment, and termination are essentially settlor functions?

IV. Summary of Testimony and Council Discussion

A. Introduction to Witnesses

The Council heard testimony from twenty-two witnesses on four different days ranging from plan sponsors, service providers, law professors, government officials, individuals and groups representing participant interests. The Council wishes to thank all of the witnesses for their insights and perspectives on the subject of de-risking and participant protections. The breadth and depth of the testimony and expertise has contributed immeasurably to this report.

The Council heard testimony from several witnesses who represent or directly service the plan sponsor community. This included one large plan sponsor, General Motors (GM), which in 2012 implemented one of the largest defined benefit risk transfers. Testifying for GM was Preston Crabill, Director of Retirement, Layoff, and Profit Sharing Plans. From the actuarial side, the Council heard from Evan Inglis from Vanguard and Craig Rosenthal from Mercer and Kent Mason (on behalf of the American Benefits Council). The Council also heard from Steve Keating from Penbridge Advisors, representing benefits consultants. His testimony focused on the reasons plan sponsors were pursuing de-risking, and specifically risk-transfer strategies. Each of these witnesses focused on the various methods by which plan sponsors implemented these strategies and issues they encountered.

Four witnesses provided testimony discussing the legal framework and its impact on de-risking transactions: Robert Newman (Covington & Burling LLP), John Ferreira (Morgan Lewis), Norman Stein (Drexel Law School), and Brendan Maher (University of Connecticut Law School).

The Council also received testimony on two different days from six witnesses representing the interests of employee, retirees, and participants. They were: Ilana Boivie, Research Economist, Communications Workers of America; Jack Cohen, Executive Vice President, BellTel Retirees; David Certner, Legislative Counsel and Legislative Policy Director, AARP; William Kadereit, President, National Retiree Legislative Network; Karin Feldman, Policy Specialist, Benefits & Social Insurance, AFL-CIO; and Karen Friedman, Executive Vice President and Policy Director, Pension Rights Center. These witnesses generally agreed that de-risking transactions placed participants' retirement security at risk for a variety of reasons and suggested numerous protections.

B. General Observations

The testimony presented to the Council is a classic case of individuals looking at the same evidence and coming to different conclusions. Much of the difference seemed to arise out of differences in perspectives as well as in experiences. However, there was a significant amount of agreement concerning the underlying drivers surrounding de-risking.

The majority of witnesses discussed a number of consistent themes. First, witnesses generally acknowledged that defined benefit pension plans are part of a voluntary pension system, albeit with important legal and contractual duties (including, where applicable, collective bargaining responsibilities) while the plan is being maintained. Second, most witnesses recognized that sponsoring a defined benefit plan can lead employers to experience volatility associated with their pension funding obligations, which can arise from factors not entirely (and sometimes not at all) within their control, with the level of volatility varying among employers and plans and sometimes in relation to the proportionate representation of active and retired participants within the plan. Third, most witnesses recognized that employers have a number of de-risking methods available to them including methods both inside and outside of the plan. Fourth, witnesses agreed that there was an essential distinction between settlor functions, where the employer makes an amendment to the plan to commence the de-risking process, and fiduciary functions, where the employer is subject to ERISA fiduciary standards to implement the de-risking process. Fifth, witnesses generally agreed that it was necessary to provide a transparent procedure by which employees would be appropriately informed of their rights during a pension de-risking process and that any such process should not interfere with employees' accrued pension rights, though there were differences among the witnesses regarding the scope and design of this procedure and process.

1. Reasons Plans are Engaging in De-risking Strategies
    a. Participants' Perspective Regarding Defined Benefit Plan De-risking

From the view of the witnesses representing participants, defined benefit plans play a meaningful role in enabling employees to realize a secure retirement. In combination with Social Security, defined benefit plans, as deferred compensation, have assisted workers in maintaining a steady income level throughout their retirement without fear of outliving their assets. Karin Feldman, Benefits and Social Insurance Policy Specialist for the AFL-CIO, supported defined benefit plans as the best means of providing meaningful secure retirement income. She highlighted several factors that she believes makes them sound and cost effective, including professional asset managers, low fees, better returns, lifetime income guarantees, and benefits to disabled workers and surviving spouses.

Although defined benefit plans provide a more secure lifetime income stream to participants, witnesses acknowledged that the number of these plans has been declining over the past few decades. Many of the plans have been frozen (partially or fully), some have been terminated, and others replaced with hybrid plans or defined contribution plans. Witnesses testifying on behalf of participants expressed a strong view that, for the majority of individuals, transferring longevity, investment and interest risks to the individual has made retirement less secure for individuals and de-risking is merely another method for transferring these risks. These same witnesses viewed de-risking accomplished within the plan, such as through purchasing bonds to match liabilities and purchasing annuities, positively. They underscored that such in-plan de-risking alternatives allow the participants to retain ERISA and PBGC protections. In contrast, they expressed concerns with de-risking which results in the participant leaving the plan (through either lump sum payments or annuities). In general, the risks which employers seek to shed are transferred to the participant, an insurance company or both. To underscore this concern, they highlighted a 2013 survey of National Retiree Legislative Network members, which indicated that 96% of those responding were extremely concerned about their financial security, especially in light of the increasing trend toward pension de-risking by plan sponsors. They are concerned that this trend will continue and accelerate the termination of defined benefit plans.

While most of the focus of the testimony of the participant witnesses was on the impact of participants removed from the plan, a number of those witnesses also reminded the Council of potential impacts on participants remaining in the plan. These witnesses were particularly concerned that the plan may become less well funded, especially if such de-risking reduced the funding level for the benefits of remaining participants. Moreover, there is always the possibility that the plan could fall below the 80% funding requirement triggering certain benefit restrictions (e.g., no increases in benefits, reduction or prohibition of new lump sum distributions) go into effect for those left in the plan. More drastically, if the plan falls to less than 60% funded, then benefit accruals must be frozen. Thus, the steps taken to de-risk could potentially have a negative impact on those participants remaining in the plan.

b. Plan Sponsors' View of Defined Benefit Plans

A consistent message from all witnesses was that those plan sponsors engaged in de-risking strategies are looking to reduce their overall exposure to their pension obligations, including the volatility in those obligations, relative to the market value, cash flows and earnings of the company. The primary risks that defined benefit plan sponsors are exposed to are the same as participants who receive a lump sum distribution: (a) interest rate risk, (b) investment and market risks, and (c) longevity risk. Witnesses also testified that plan sponsors face regulatory obligations, risks and administrative costs for maintaining the plan.

i. Disconnect between the plan and the company's current mission

For many plan sponsors, their defined benefit plans are closed to new entrants and/or have frozen accruals for current covered employees. For some companies, the size of the pension obligation is very large and thus has a disproportionate effect on the company's balance sheet. Because of the plan sponsor's view that these obligations are a legacy cost, are not a core company focus for workforce management, and can expose the plan sponsor to significant risks, the testimony indicated that plan sponsors are looking to reduce or remove these risk exposures in the most efficient way possible, while still honoring their legal obligations to pay retirees and their beneficiaries the full benefits earned.

GM illustrates these circumstances. Preston Crabill, GM's Director of Retirement, Layoff, and Profit Sharing Plans, testified that given the changes in auto manufacturing, GM is a smaller company than it once was; yet the amount of its legacy defined benefit obligations are still large. He noted that, although GM had relatively well-funded pension plans, it faced the annual risk that relatively small changes in interest rates or plan actuarial losses (through unexpectedly lower investment returns or otherwise) would create large and disproportionate balance sheet losses and significant funding obligations to its defined benefit pension plans.

ii. Changes to accounting standards and funding rules have increased volatility

Given that plan sponsors engage in de-risking strategies to reduce the impact of volatility in their obligations and funded status, witnesses pointed to legislative and regulatory changes in defined benefit funding rules, as well as changes to accounting standards, as being significant drivers of de-risking decisions. Funding rules and accounting standards require more mark-to-market valuation of assets and liabilities, greater recognition of pension obligations, and funding gaps to be closed more quickly. Thus, the consequence of these risks on pension obligations are felt more quickly, both in terms of cash flow requirements and the financial condition of the plan and plan sponsor.

Witnesses agreed that the Pension Protection Act of 2006 (PPA) has provided the biggest impetus for plans to use de-risking strategies. Among its many provisions, the PPA reduced the smoothing that plans were allowed to use to value their liabilities and their assets, so that volatility in interest rates and the investment portfolio were felt much more quickly in terms of the calculated funded ratio. Further, the PPA set forth higher funding requirements, requiring plans to reach 100% funding within an accelerated period of time relative to requirements prior to its enactment. Finally, the PPA prohibits plans that fall below 80% of the funded ratio from paying out lump sums; those plans that fall below 60% funded ratio must freeze all accruals. Not surprisingly, witnesses testified that plan sponsors did not want to fall below these thresholds.

Witnesses agreed that the Financial Accounting Standards Board (FASB) rules also requiring greater mark-to-market valuation of pension obligations and greater recognition of these obligations on financial statements were significant drivers toward de-risking strategies. Craig Rosenthal from Mercer testified that although FAS-87 mandated that pension costs appear in a company's income statement using prescribed methodologies, for the most part those were based on corporate bond rates and were usually found only in the footnotes of the balance sheet. However, the implementation of FAS-158 in 2006 brought mark-to-market accounting of the pension obligations directly to the balance sheet. Mr. Rosenthal testified that it is anticipated that FASB will implement other requirements to bring accounting standards in the United States more in line with international standards.

At the time new funding and accounting requirements were implemented, as Evan Inglis from Vanguard testified, there was significant volatility in the financial markets. Although interest rates used to value plan pension liabilities have been declining for the last 30 years, the increased cost in pension obligations were masked by very strong market returns, particularly from the equity markets. However, in the early 2000s, interest rates and the equity markets dropped in tandem, with significant negative consequences for plan funding levels. In 2008, both interest rate and equity market returns again fell in tandem with similar results for plan funding. During both periods, plan sponsors were required not only to fund up their plans in a period of economic slowdown, but also to report higher liabilities and expenses to shareholders. These pension obligations were increasingly viewed as legacy costs, sometimes for a growing block of former employees with no role in ensuring the organization's future success. Facing growing levels of market volatility and accounting and regulatory changes, plan sponsors increased their efforts to identify strategies to mitigate and transfer risk.

iii. Favorable interest rate for lump sum calculations

If a defined benefit pension plan offers a lump sum option in lieu of the annuity, these two distribution options must be actuarially equivalent. The PPA revised the method by which actuarial equivalence was calculated for lump sums. Prior to the PPA, lump sums were valued based on a Treasury interest rate, which was lower than corporate bond interest rates used to value the plan liabilities for funding purposes. Witnesses noted that lower interest rates generally result in less discounting of the pension obligation in determining the lump sum value, thus making the lump sums larger and more expensive to the plan. The PPA change to corporate bond rates meant higher discounting rates and thus lower lump sum obligations for the plan. Witnesses noted that prior to PPA, the lump sum could be more than the amount carried as a liability for funding purposes and thus the lump sum payout would negatively impact the funding ratio. However, the PPA rate changes, which were phased in from 2006 to 2012, more closely matched the liability interest rate. Consequently, calendar year 2012 saw heightened activity by plan sponsors in offering lump sum payouts. Plans could pay out lump sums, reducing the size of their obligations, at a lower cost than before the PPA changes.

Not only was 2012 the first year for full phase-in of the lump sum rates, but federal tax rules, which were in existence prior to PPA, allowed the plan to use a 5-month look back rule to set the interest rates used to value lump sums. In 2012, as rates were declining, this rule allowed plans to look back to higher rates as early as August 2011, and thus to pay out smaller lump sums than if they had been required to use more current rates. Witnesses maintained this was a one-time opportunity, as the same federal tax rules also limit the plan's ability to change the methodology for determining the lump sum interest rate.

Witnesses representing the employer and consulting communities emphasized that current de-risking strategies are aimed at reducing the volatility of a plan sponsor's liability. Some of them also argued that pursuing de-risking strategies was critical to the defined benefit system and could actually be helpful in allowing employers to continue to maintain plans for participants still working for employers. Some witnesses believed that if funding levels increase due to better markets and/or higher interest rates used to discount liabilities, de-risking could become more affordable and the number of transactions might accelerate, potentially leading to additional de-risking transactions.

iv. Other factors

Witnesses also testified that PBGC premiums have become more significant and less predictable over the last few years with proposals to significantly increase these premiums. In addition, similar to PBGC premiums, other costs such as recordkeeping are assessed on a per capita basis. Witnesses suggested that one benefit of de-risking, particularly payment of lump sums to terminated deferred vested participants, is to reduce the number of covered participants, thus reducing costs.

Finally, some witnesses pointed to anticipated changes in longevity tables used to value their liabilities. Given the expected increase in longevity used to value liabilities, plan sponsors believe that not only will lump sums be more expensive in the future, but the size of the plan liabilities used to calculate the plan's funding obligations and reported on financial statements will also increase.

c. Perspective of the Regulators and the Guarantors

Testimony of witnesses representing the regulators and the guarantors provided important insight and perspective on the reasons for de-risking and echoed some of the same concerns and perspectives expressed by other witnesses.

i. EBSA

Joe Canary, Director of the Office of Regulations and Interpretations, EBSA, presented the Council with an overview of the issues surrounding de-risking strategies. He highlighted a number of issues that are implicit in de-risking transactions. These included the distinctions between settlor and fiduciary functions; selection of an annuity provider; participant communications; and the importance of lifetime income streams for participants.

ii. Pension Benefit Guaranty Corporation (PBGC)

Josh Gotbaum, Director (CEO) of the PBGC, provided an important perspective on a number of the concerns noted by other witnesses. He observed that current rules appear to incent plans to de-risk and to do so disproportionately with lump sums, because of a combination of regulatory hurdles and cost advantages. He suggested that lump sums are inappropriate for many participants, and likened pension plan lump-sum cash-outs to cigarettes: legal, liked, and bad for you. He also opined that he would like to see fewer incentives for participants to choose lump sum distributions. One suggestion was less criticism of annuities, which might be (unintentionally) causing more individuals to elect a lump sum. To further make the point, he stated that he did not think that a defined benefit plan with a PBGC guarantee was necessarily safer than an insurance company annuity backed by a state insurance guaranty association.

iii. Insurance regulators and state guaranty funds

These witnesses focused on the multiple layers of protections in the insurance and regulatory oversight, as well as the state guaranty protections that provide a further backstop to the interests of plan participants for whom the annuities are purchased. The testimony of Philip Barlow, from the District of Columbia Department of Insurance, Securities and Banking, echoed the general message of Mr. Gotbaum's observations about the relative strength of insurance oversight and protections. He emphasized: NAIC accreditations; restrictions on investment types, investment concentration, and investment valuation; holding company rules; review of material transactions; and the NAIC Financial Analysis Working Group (FAWG) peer review process. The testimony highlighted the regulatory scrutiny of an insurance company's ability to deliver on their obligations of various durations.

Peter Gallanis, from the National Organization of Life and Health Guaranty Associations, testified regarding the strength of the state guaranty funds. The state funds provide a benefit floor, or minimum, with additional benefits payable in excess of the floor based on the level of available insurance company assets in the liquidation. By contrast, PBGC guarantees provide a cap, or upper limit, on the benefits being guaranteed. For both PBGC and state guaranty funds, most participants have benefits below the cap and within the range of the state guarantees. Nevertheless, as he noted, the facts regarding the different federal and state guarantees remain important.

Providing additional perspective, Mr. Gallanis also highlighted a stark contrast between, on the one hand, the hundreds of defined benefit plans that failed during the great recession, and the many companies that failed or received government assistance, with, on the other hand, only six insurance companies, with combined assets under $800 million, that went into liquidation under the state guaranty system during the same period, with most policyholders paid in full. He also noted the favorable discussion of this record in the recent Government Accountability Office report on this same favorable performance of the industry during the economic turmoil of 2008 and thereafter.

2. Methods of De-risking

Testimony established that employers de-risk their pension obligations using a number of internal and external approaches, with internal methods permitting the plan sponsor to reduce many (but not all) of its risks while leaving the participants in the plan. In-plan strategies include restricting participation or accruals, hedging and immunization (both considered liability-driven investing (LDI)), and buy-ins. Options for de-risking outside of the plan, and permanently discharging the employer's obligations, include lump sum offers, buy-outs, and plan termination (including "spin offs"). This section of the report reviews some of the primary approaches currently in use.

a) Freezing Eligibility or Benefits

Witnesses testified that the first step most plans take to lower plan liabilities is to slow or stop future benefit accruals in the plan. Such measures include closing the plan to new entrants; reducing the benefit formula, either for all participants or for new employees; and freezing the plan's future accruals. One or more of these strategies may be undertaken in tandem with the introduction or expansion of a defined contribution plan for some or all of the plan sponsor's eligible employees or the offering of no employer sponsored retirement plan at all. These measures will slow or stop the growth of the defined benefit plan's obligations, possibly replacing them with a new, more predictable contribution obligation for the defined contribution plan. Such steps, however, leave the existing pension benefit promises subject to volatility in interest rates and longevity, perhaps for many years. According to Steve Keating of Penbridge Advisors, roughly one-third of defined benefit plans are frozen today (participants receive no benefit accrual or use of increased salary in the formula). And Vanguard's Evan Inglis also noted that many of these frozen plans ultimately wind up being terminated.

b) Liability Driven Investing (LDI)

Witnesses testified that given the impact of the PPA, as well as the funding rules and accounting standards with the greater use of mark-to-market valuation of liabilities and assets, plans have looked to reduce the volatility in funded ratios by more closely matching the characteristics of their assets with their liabilities. Asset-liability matching is a familiar concept for many businesses, especially regulated businesses generally and insurance companies specifically.

Pension liabilities are valued using a market-based interest rate. Because of the long duration of pension obligations, many plans have a liability duration that often averages 10 years or longer. Longer durations mean that changes in interest rates can have a correspondingly large impact on the value of the liabilities.

Plans implement an LDI strategy to attempt to get more exposure in their portfolio to the types of interest rate risks that correspond to their liabilities. In order to match risks to liabilities, plans increase the total duration of the portfolio by investing in more bonds, longer duration bonds, and bonds with specific characteristics more closely corresponding to the plan's liabilities. While this can help mute the impact of the interest rate risk to plan sponsors, it does not remove the obligations or eliminate all risks and costs to continue the plan. Moreover, LDI may be better suited to larger plans that have the ability to spread such risks across larger numbers of participants than to smaller plans, where variations among a small number of participants can have a disproportionate impact on the plan's funding status.

c) Liabilities Transferred to Insurance Company

In order to further reduce a plan's exposure to the various risks described earlier, the Council received a significant amount of testimony concerning plan sponsors who have chosen to transfer the plan's risks to an insurance company through the purchase of an annuity that matches the payout obligations to the participant. By purchasing the annuity, the insurance company bears the same risks as the plan did: interest rate risk, investment and market risks, and longevity risk. Plan sponsors can either purchase annuities to be held within the plan, or distribute them out of the plan.

In-plan annuities, often referred to as "buy-ins," become a plan asset. Nothing else changes: the plan participant remains a participant covered under ERISA; the plan still pays the participant; plan sponsors continue to pay administrative costs and PBGC premiums for that individual. Such purchases can reduce or eliminate the volatility of the plan's investments, replacing them with the contract's guarantees. If purchased with respect to vested benefits of former employees, buy-ins can function much like the buyout alternative discussed below. In a buy-in, the plan continues to pay for both the protection of the annuity contract and the protection of PBGC guarantees. Thus far, annuity buy-ins have been very rare in this country, although they have been more popular in other countries such as the United Kingdom.

A buy-out occurs when the plan discharges its obligation by transferring its risk to the insurer by purchasing annuities for the participants. Such purchases, when made outside of the context of a plan termination, generally include the vested benefits of a group of former employees. In two large recent cases (GM, Verizon), the purchase included employees who already had started receiving retirement benefits from the plan.

Following the purchase, the participants' rights and protections are circumscribed by the annuity contract, the financial status of the issuer, and the state guaranty fund protections; in place of the protections of PBGC coverage and the provisions of ERISA (though some ERISA provisions may be incorporated into the contract). Once the transaction is complete, the participant will receive an annuity certificate from the insurance company, will receive payments from that insurer, and will be protected through the state insurance system and state guaranty associations.

As a corollary, the plan sponsor no longer has any ERISA obligations or associated costs. Mr. Keating highlighted a number of possible advantages to the plan sponsor in transferring risk, including: lowering their risk profile; improving their competitive position; removing uncertainty around pension expense; producing more consistent financial results; focusing on their core business; and taking comfort that a highly credit worthy company is taking responsibility for making future payments to transferred participants. Possible disadvantages associated with annuity buyouts included: the loss of liquidity; the increase in leverage associated with purchase costs; and the negative impact on earnings due to settlement accounting.

As noted by EBSA's Joe Canary, the primary DOL guidance regarding annuity purchases by defined benefit pension plans is IB 95-1, which sets forth multiple factors to be considered by a plan fiduciary (but not safe harbors) with respect to such purchases. The process requires that the plan fiduciary either possess the requisite expertise or engage one or more third parties to provide it. Because of the complexity required in evaluating annuity providers and the structure of the contract, the Council heard testimony regarding the use of consultants and independent fiduciaries to assist in the transaction and the selection of the annuity provider. Mr. Crabill stated that GM relied heavily on the factors listed in IB 95-1. Mr. Crabill testified that GM used an annuity committee to select the independent fiduciary to assume responsibility for the fiduciary decisions described in IB 95-1. He noted that the independent fiduciary, State Street, in turn engaged Oliver Wyman, to advise on the selection of the insurer, including a review of an insurer candidate's capability and safety, and the structure of the insurance contract.

Among other approaches plan sponsors weigh is the use of a single insurance company or multiple insurers to provide the annuities. Mr. Crabill testified that although GM, through its advisors, considered using multiple insurers, their consultants concluded that a single carrier supported by a separate account contract structure was an appropriate choice to protect the interests and benefits of the retirees.

Costs to purchase annuities can vary. Mr. Inglis testified that generally annuities are 5% to 15% higher than the value of the same pension promises under the plan. The higher cost of the annuities generally reflects more conservative discount rates used by the insurer, higher longevity assumptions used by the insurer compared with plan assumptions, and insurance company profits. Witnesses testified that the purchase is still often cost effective for the plan in light of the elimination of administrative costs and PBGC liabilities for those annuitants.

On a historical note, Mr. Keating of Penbridge Advisors stated that in the United States the annual amount of annuity buy-outs has typically been less than $3 billion over the last twenty years; it stood at less than $1 billion annually for recent years before 2012. In 2012, he testified that 98% of all transactions were less than $250 million, with most less than $10 million. However, two of the largest annuity purchases in history occurred in 2012 when GM and Verizon purchased combined $33.6 billion dollars in annuity contracts to settle their liabilities for a large portion of their pension participants.

d) Liabilities Transferred to the Individual

While plan sponsors can transfer their pension obligation risks to an insurance company, they can also transfer their risks through lump sum payments to the participants and beneficiaries. The plan pays to the participant or beneficiary a single payment based on the present value of the promised annuity. Testimony confirmed that defined benefit pension plans are permitted to include lump sum features in their plan, subject to funding adequacy requirements, and that many plans already include such lump sum options, which may be available at any time or only at specific times, such as severance from service or upon attaining retirement age. Nevertheless, testimony also noted that recent developments indicate an increasing incidence of introduction or expansion of lump sum provisions, including lump sum options offered to retirees in pay status.

The Council heard testimony that lump sum distributions can be less expensive to the plan than annuity purchases or maintaining the benefit under the plan, particularly for younger former employees. (Neither lump sums nor annuity purchases are likely to be available to active participants who are continuing to accrue benefits under the plan.) Particularly for those participants with small balances, lump sum distributions reduce the fixed costs associated with administration and PBGC premiums. There was testimony that the offering lump sums could result in anti-selection bias. Those participants who believe they have a lower life expectancy than average, perhaps due to illness or genetic disposition, will elect to take the lump sum, leaving those with higher life expectancies in the plan.

Plans have implemented the lump sum strategy in various ways, frequently by offering the lump sum to a particular group in the plan. By far the most common strategy is to offer a lump sum option to terminated deferred vested participants during an election window. In this scenario, participants and beneficiaries are offered the opportunity to elect a lump sum of their vested benefit if they make a selection within a 60 or 90-day period. Mr. Rosenthal of Mercer estimates that there is a 40-60% take-up rate, which frequently correlates with age, with younger participants being less likely to elect the lump sum. He also saw a positive correlation between the size of the lump sum and the decision to directly roll it over to a tax deferred vehicle (i.e., the larger the amount of the lump sum, the more likely it would be rolled over to an individual retirement account).

A less frequently used strategy is to offer lump sum distributions to retirees already in pay status. In the case of Ford and GM, in 2012 each company received a special letter ruling from the IRS that permitted them to offer certain retirees who were in pay status the ability to elect to receive the remaining present value of their pension payments in the form of a lump sum without violating distribution requirements in the federal tax code. Mr. Crabill testified that GM offered the lump sum option to 44,000 retirees and their surviving spouses. He said that the take up rate was about 30%, resulting in approximately $3.6 billion in lump sum payments.

In order to implement a lump sum window, plan sponsors may hire one or more service providers such as an actuary, a participant investment advisor and/or a benefit consultant.

These providers help the plan sponsor determine whether, and if so how to, offer such a lump sum window; and to calculate the lump sum amounts and interface with the participants through communications, websites, call centers and in-person meetings. (Similar functions can be involved in decisions by a plan sponsor to include a more general lump sum feature in the plan, as well as to calculate individual lump sums.) Witnesses representing or servicing the plan sponsor community acknowledged that the choice of a lump sum does transfer all the associated interest, market and longevity risks to the individual, who now must manage the money themselves or work with an advisor. They also acknowledged that lump sum payouts are not always required to include the value of an early retirement subsidy, which is another cost-savings to the plan and a disadvantage to the recipient. The Council received conflicting testimony as to whether current rules already require the disclosure of the presence or absence of this subsidy in the lump sum calculations.

3. Other Issues Plans/Plan Sponsors Consider In De-Risking Transactions

a) Settlement accounting

Some transactions, specifically those that involve plan terminations, require "settlement accounting." Mr. Keating testified that many plans have substantial unrecognized actuarial losses, classified as accumulated other comprehensive income/loss. When a plan is terminated, the company needs to immediately recognize any losses on its financial statements. The testimony was mixed on plan sponsor's reactions to this requirement. Some plans want to avoid any impact on their financial statements, so they will consider approaches like lump sum windows and annuity buy-ins. Other plans are willing to show losses on their statements, but would rather do it all at once.

b) Liquidity and Characteristics of the Defined Benefit Plan After the Risk Transfer

The Council heard testimony on the impact of risk transfer strategies on the plan and remaining participants. Longevity increases, interest rate sensitivities, liquidity in the remaining plan assets and reduced amount of assets, all may impact the plan, resulting in, among other things, changes to the duration of the plan and a negative impact on the funded status of the plan.

c) Data Clean-up

Several witnesses testified about the importance of making sure plan data was "clean" before conducting a risk transfer transaction. This includes making sure addresses are correct, beneficiary information is up to date, and employment records are accurate. This data is important in terms of communicating to participants and making sure liabilities are valued accurately.

d) Fiduciary v. Settlor Functions

With regard to the legal framework surrounding these pension de-risking strategies, the testimony established that the appropriate framework shifted based on whether it was an in-plan or external strategy. In-plan strategies are a plan investment, so plan sponsors have fiduciary obligations, including the obligations to act in the best interests of plan participants and beneficiaries as well as with a duty of care consistent with a prudent fiduciary in similar circumstances. In particular, it was noted that DOL Advisory Opinion 2006-08A addresses fiduciary obligations in the context of liability-driven investing and states that, "nothing in ERISA limits a planned fiduciary's ability to take into account the risks associated with benefits liabilities." In contrast, the decision to pursue an out-of-plan de-risking strategy is a matter of plan design and is thus a settlor function (though this settlor distinction was criticized by Professor Stein where the plan design decision clearly harms the plan's participants). Under the settlor-function doctrine, such decision-making by plan sponsors is not subject to ERISA fiduciary requirements. Once the plan sponsor has decided to pursue an external de-risking strategy, the implementation of that strategy is again subject to fiduciary obligations.

The Council heard testimony from several witnesses on how plan sponsors manage their fiduciary duties and obligations. Witnesses testified concerning the necessity of being clear in what capacity the individual is acting and the use of outside advisors and independent fiduciaries to support them. For example, Mr. Crabill testified that GM hired an independent fiduciary in recognition of this potential conflict to assist in negotiating with the insurance company. To further separate functions, GM also decided that those who hired the independent fiduciary would not be involved in the negotiations.

e) Participant Protections

Witnesses generally agreed that it was necessary to provide a transparent procedure by which employees would be appropriately informed of their rights during a pension de-risking process. Significantly, all witnesses agreed that any such process should not interfere with employees' accrued pension rights. There was, however, disagreement about the scope and design of this procedure and process.

f) Annuities

Participant witnesses raised various concerns when a plan sponsor de-risks through the purchase of annuities. First, such de-risking effectively ends any PBGC and ERISA fiduciary protections of a participant's benefits following the transaction, replacing them instead with the contractual protections of the annuity contract, the regulatory protections of state insurance law regulation and oversight, and a state guaranty backstop if, and when, the first two fail. Moreover, when a participant has been transferred from a defined benefit plan to a private annuity, that participant no longer has the protections of ERISA, such as fiduciary duty and annual disclosure reports, but instead must rely on the terms of the annuity contract. In addition, while ERISA protects the qualified pension benefits from claims of creditors, testimony to the Council was not definitive as to the extent to which states, as well as current bankruptcy laws, similarly protect annuity payments.

Second, while the life insurance companies from which annuities currently are being purchased are generally viewed as financially strong, in the past even some companies which have been viewed as financially solid have gotten into financial difficulty. Participant witnesses pointed to the dramatic events of 2008 that led to the government bail-out of large banks and corporations, and the failure of Lehman Brothers. Participant witnesses also pointed to the 1991 failure of Executive Life (which, as noted by other witnesses, also pre-dated much of the enhanced insurance regulatory oversight of the past two decades).

Nevertheless, it was also true that the ratings companies had given Executive Life stellar ratings until shortly before it collapsed, and it took years to sort out compensation to those insureds.

Participant witnesses noted that state guaranty funds are not advance-funded. Moreover, the specific amounts of state guarantees depend on the insured's state of residence and the amount of state guarantees vary, with all states providing a base amount of guarantees and many states, having adopted newer NAIC models, providing higher guarantees. If both were to be viewed as a ceiling on the benefits payable, the most protective of the state guarantees would be less than that provided by PBGC. This variance in state guarantees leads to the possibility that two annuitants – equal in all respects except for the states in which they live – could experience very different levels of protection. However, as noted by Mr. Gallanis, state guarantees serve as a floor, rather than a ceiling, with annuitants frequently recovering well in excess of the floor amounts identified in the state guarantees. He noted specifically that high levels of state and NAIC oversight, including early intervention while the company's assets still cover much and perhaps all of their obligations ("asset coverage percentage") could result both in annuitants receiving their full benefit, even in excess of the benefit guaranteed by PBGC, through the combination of state guaranty minimums and the additional asset coverage percentage.

Another question that was raised regarding annuity purchases was market capacity. Two participant witnesses questioned whether insurance companies had sufficient capacity to absorb a continued surge in de-risking activity as a result of the historically large annuity purchases by GM. The Council received limited testimony on this question, neither favorable nor unfavorable, other than noting that (a) capacity may expand to meet demand; and (b) insurance regulatory oversight was likely to provide early indicators of potential capacity issues for an individual company.

A number of participant witnesses also asked how disputes are handled, particularly mistakes made during the purchase of the annuity contract. One example was: Who will be responsible if the participant's age or service is incorrect and what impact will this have on the participant's benefit? Witnesses noted that some annuity contracts clearly addressed these types of questions and encouraged others to do so as well. Participant witnesses also expressed concerns that the insurance company itself might take steps to de-risk, such as offering a lump sum to the annuitants, although other witnesses noted that this would require a contract provision from the outset. If this should occur, the participant witnesses questioned how the lump sum amount would be calculated, what disclosures would be required, and whether spousal consent would be necessary.

Professor Maher did not believe that any and all de-risking transactions are necessarily a bad deal for beneficiaries merely because of the loss of PBGC and fiduciary protections, and that state guarantees, whether old or new, plus state contract law on remedies, could be as attractive or more attractive to employees.

g. Lump Sum Distributions

Participant witnesses generally focused on two de-risking alternatives – lump sum distributions and annuity purchases. Many participant witnesses regard lump sum distributions as less desirable than an annuity, except in the unusual situation where the individual and the spouse have a short life expectancy. The reasons for this disfavor are not new, but have been supported by these witnesses' own experiences.

Participant witnesses echoed one central conclusion, which they believed many participants do not understand. A lump sum comes with many of the risks which caused the employer to de-risk in the first instance – the risk of investment losses, the failure to meet investment objectives and the risk of outliving the invested lump sum. Added to this is the risk the monies will be spent early on non-retirement purchases and thus will not be available when needed for their retirement.

Participant witnesses stated that most participants do not have the understanding, experience, or expertise to manage investments or even select an investment advisor, especially in comparison to a plan's investment manager. Moreover, because a participant's investment time frame is shorter than that of a plan, they are less able to weather the volatility of the markets. Further, because participants are individuals, they are likely to pay more for investment advice and asset management, thereby leaving them with less for the long term. There is neither a PBGC guarantee nor a state guarantee associated with a lump sum distribution. In addition, participants considering receipt of a lump sum must consider carefully the personal tax consequences, both at the time of the receipt and afterwards.

Some participant witnesses assisted retirees in pay status who recently had been offered lump sum distributions. These witnesses observed that these offers caused great distress and anxiety among the retirees. These retirees often had taken their time to plan their retirement and now had to decide, in a short period of time, whether to accept a lump sum. The witnesses noted that some of those making these decisions were old, more vulnerable to pressure from relatives and investment advisors and, in some cases, diminished in their capacity to weigh the pros and cons of the options.

Because of the interest rate assumptions defined benefit plans are now allowed to use in their calculation of lump sums (which plan sponsors have argued are more consistent with the assumptions for funding the plan), the amount of the lump sum is less than the participants would have received if the prior interest rate rules from previous years were in effect. "Indeed," as NLRN observed, "it's no coincidence that the first large-scale lump sum buy-out offers (GM and Ford) occurred in 2012, since that is when the Pension Protection Act's less generous lump sum calculation were fully phased in." In addition, the law permits a plan to exclude the amount of an early retirement subsidy in the lump sum calculation even when an individual would receive the subsidy in an annuity from the plan. This aspect engendered much discussion among the Council. David Certner of AARP stated that in order to choose the lump sum offer participants generally had to choose the option against their best interests.

The Council heard broadly divergent opinions over the desirability of such lump sums being offered, especially to retirees already receiving annuities. Some witnesses thought it was best to give employee and retirees options, allowing them to make decisions based on their specific needs and circumstances, and thought employees could make the appropriate choices given the right information. And one retiree testified that he should have been given the option of a lump sum, but was not. In contrast, others referred to lump sums as "the devil," and the offering of lump sums to current retirees already receiving plan pensions as "corporate elder abuse" and "the most cynical and worst of all pension abuses that have emerged post-ERISA." For his part, Professor Stein testified that, everyone besides those who are terminally ill, or almost everyone else who selects a lump sum, will be forfeiting a substantial portion of their retirement savings. He based his comments on conclusions from some behavioral economists, that individuals have difficulty accurately discounting future payments and thus over-value lump sums. Another issue raised by some of the witnesses was the role of a financial advisor in providing education or recommendations regarding the lump sum option and the extent to which any advice (as contrasted with education) could involve a conflicting interest in favor of the lump sum.

C. Discussion of Proposed Recommendations to the Council

Witnesses offered numerous and divergent recommendations, ranging from take no action, to disallowing one or more (or all) de-risking transactions, and many proposals in between.

Two of the legal witnesses who represented employers (Mr. Newman and Mr. Ferreira) favored a minimalistic approach. While not eschewing all regulation, Mr. Newman suggested any future guidance should be practical, should be necessary, and should be done while keeping in mind what ERISA already requires of fiduciaries and that such obligations do not mandate a single result. Mr. Ferreira, based on his belief that his clients and most employers seek to do right by their employees in these circumstances, suggested that caution be exercised before DOL take any regulatory actions since defined benefit plans already "have been regulated out of existence."

Participant witnesses made numerous suggestions concerning potential participant protections in the case of annuity purchases, intended to improve the transparency of the transaction to the participants, including:

- Require participant consent to an annuity distribution; Clarify the "safest annuity" obligations under IB 95-1;
- Provide further guidance on what constitutes a thorough investigation and analysis of an annuity and what standards constitute "safest" available annuity;
- Redefine the annuity selection standard to the "most protective" annuity, and/or require a third party to certify the qualifying annuity providers;
- Require use of a separate account for purchased annuity contracts;
- Require reinsurance for purchased annuity obligations, potentially from the PBGC; Restrict the annuity issuer from unilaterally offering lump sum options;
- Require annuity contracts to include protections against garnishment and attachment by creditors or bankruptcy trustees; and
- Develop dispute resolution process in the event a participant has a dispute.

A number of these recommendations were incorporated in whole or part into the Council's recommendations, while others were either answered by other witnesses or simply were not accepted by the Council. For example, other witnesses noted that neither ERISA nor the Code provided authority to prohibit lump sums or to impose a consent requirement on annuity purchases, although it was noted that some plans provide participants with an election between a lump sum and an annuity distribution at retirement. Witnesses also noted that IB 95-1 already includes separate accounts as a factor to consider under the safest available annuity standard; the Council noted that the same considerations involved in large plans like GM are not necessarily applicable or appropriate for all plans. Additionally, Mr. Gotbaum noted that the PBGC does not have authority to provide reinsurance to insurers.

The Council heard testimony from opposing positions on the question of whether the DOL should provide for a notice and comment period prior to acting on proposals for additional guidance on (1) fiduciary/settlor functions in these transactions, (2) expansion of IB 95-1, and (3) needed participant disclosures relating to elections of lump sum distributions. The Council unanimously agreed that any such changes should be made prospectively only.

With respect to the form of guidance, Council members recognize that the administrative process for determining how guidance should be issued is in the purview of the Department. The Council members also recognize the importance of obtaining input from the public, particularly with respect to significant changes in existing law. At the same time, the Council recognizes that immediate guidance might be needed in certain areas.

In situations where plans de-risk by offering participants lump sum pay-outs, some of the witnesses representing participants recommended that DOL should:

- Require plans to make independent, non-conflicted, objective advice available to participants;
- Require steps to be taken to mitigate and prevent undue influence; and Prohibit the offering of lump sum buy-outs to retired participants.

Other witnesses noted, however, that a plan is not required to provide specific education or advice, and that existing prohibited transaction guidance already imposes requirements for avoiding or eliminating conflicts in the case of advice. Other more general suggestions were that DOL should:

- Issue guidance to clarify that any worsening of plan funding by virtue of de-risking is a fiduciary violation;
- Require disclosure of the impact of de-risking on other benefits, such as retiree health insurance;

- Require adequate protection of spousal rights; and
- Require reporting to the federal government of all de-risking transactions.

The majority of witnesses agreed that plans and plan sponsors should be transparent with the plan participants and include appropriate disclosures. The Council heard a significant amount of testimony concerning the types, content, and timing of disclosures.

Where a participant is offered a choice between an annuity and a lump sum, participant witnesses stressed the importance of full and complete disclosure to participants of the pros and cons of the choices they are being offered and adequate time to make this vitally important decision. Bill Kadereit of NLRN suggested that DOL clarify fiduciary responsibilities to include providing thorough plain English disclosures concerning the financial trade-offs, including tax consequences and the higher cost of purchasing an individual annuity contract. Karin Feldman of the AFL-CIO suggested that checklists of issues or worksheets might be helpful. Karen Friedman of the Pension Rights Center urged that disclosure requirements be made more robust, in order to caution retirees against investment risks, tax consequences, loss of federal insurance protections, and the consequences of waiving spousal benefits. David Certner of AARP argued that participants should receive disclosures about how much less they will typically receive with a lump sum than an annuity or pension. These witnesses agreed that DOL should test any draft documents to ensure they are appropriately designed and understandable.

Participant witnesses asserted that such disclosures should be sent in paper form, by mail, and not electronically. The Council heard testimony from plans and plan sponsors agreeing with this suggestion; most plans scrubbed their data prior to the transaction to ensure it would have accurate addresses. Participants would be notified by a post card that information about the de-risking transaction would be forthcoming. This also gave plans an opportunity to update addresses again. If there was a lump sum offer, it was sent in paper form, by mail, because that was the delivery method to which the most participants were the most likely to respond.

Participant groups suggested that the content of the disclosures should include:

- Pros and cons of lump sum offers including an explanation of interest, investment and longevity risks;

- The value of the lump sum being offered as compared to the value of the promised pension benefit. By so doing this should quantify the amount the participant would "lose" (if applicable) by taking the lump sum;
- An indication whether an early retirement subsidy is included in the calculation of the lump sum, and if not, the value of the lost early retirement subsidy;
- The fact that the PBGC is no longer insuring the pension; Any tax consequences of accepting a lump sum; and Any spousal notices and required consents.

Even if the de-risking transaction did not require participants to make a choice, such as the transfer of their annuity to an insurer, the participant witnesses believed that participants should receive certain disclosures so that they would understand the transaction and the potential problems if the insurer should become insolvent.

Participant witnesses felt strongly that, given the consequences of the decisions being made, the amount of time afforded in the recent high profile transactions was inadequate. Mr. Certner suggested that participants should have at least 30 days' notice that an option is going to be offered, then at least 90 days to make a decision and at least one or two weeks cooling off period, similar to the Age Discrimination in Employment Act (ADEA), in which they can change that decision.

IV. Rationale for Council Recommendations

A. IB 95-1

DOL IB 95-1 sets forth six factors that fiduciaries should consider when selecting an annuity provider for such a transaction. DOL has referred to this obligation as one to select the "safest available annuity" unless under the circumstances it would be in the interest of participants and beneficiaries to do otherwise. Relying solely on ratings provided by insurance rating services is not sufficient. Testimony raised questions about the applicability of IB 95-1 to plan de-risking transactions (although testimony from EBSA seemed to presume that it applied), and also noted the absence of safe harbors in IB 95-1. Testimony also noted additional considerations that might be considered for such safe harbors, in addition to those already listed in IB 95-1. The Council agreed that these additional factors may be appropriate for inclusion in one or more safe harbors, along with existing factors outlined in IB 95-1. The Council agreed unanimously that all guidance should be clearly prospective in its application.

B. Disclosures

Based on the testimony from numerous stakeholders, it became clear to the Council that comprehensive and accurate disclosures are essential so that participants and beneficiaries have all of the information necessary to make informed decisions concerning their choice between a lump sum distribution and an annuity (whether under the plan or through an insurer). Understanding longevity, investment, and interest risks are crucial to making this informed decision. This information is particularly important for those participants already in pay status because of the potential financial and emotional impact of the decision process. Of course, plan communications must be objective, and not biased by the employer's objective of accomplishing the de-risking transaction, in order for the plan fiduciaries to meet their fiduciary obligations. In this connection, the Council has recommended that the disclosure include an "apples to apples" comparison of the dollar value of the lump sum distribution to the dollar value of the benefit otherwise payable under the plan or under a purchased annuity contract. The Council contemplates a comparison similar to that proposed under the IRS regulation governing disclosures of relative values.

Three issues were of particular concern to the Council. The first was whether participants understand that if they are eligible for an early retirement subsidy when they chose an annuity, they could lose that subsidy if they chose a lump sum distribution. For some participants, that amount could be substantial. Consequently, the Council has recommended that disclosures include a statement as to whether an early retirement subsidy was included in the calculation of a lump sum distribution (for those plans that offer such a subsidy).

The second issue was whether participants' understood if tax penalties were due on past annuity distributions. Clearly, any tax consequences may have a significant impact on their choice. Thus, the Council recommends that this tax information be provided to participants.

A third issue was that participants and participant groups testified that generally 60 days was insufficient time to make an informed decision. The

Council agrees that participants and beneficiaries should receive disclosures at least 90 days prior to any transaction occurring in order to ensure that participants and beneficiaries have adequate time to make an informed decision. This is particularly important for those participants in pay status.

On a more general note, the Council suggests that DOL consider holding focus groups among affected participants to determine which disclosures and what formats are the most helpful to participants. The Department should test draft disclosures to ensure they are appropriately designed and understandable.

C. Fiduciary Liability for Annuity Selection

ERISA Section 502(a)(9) provides that a participant, beneficiary, a plan fiduciary, or DOL may bring a civil action for appropriate relief, including the issuance of a security bond for the harm caused by the fiduciary breach. Section 502(a)(9) accomplishes two important purposes: (1) it requires employers to follow fiduciary standards in purchasing annuities for participants and beneficiaries of the plan; and (2) where the fiduciary standard is breached, it provides a remedy.

A majority of the Council believes that fiduciaries and plan sponsors would be assisted if the Department provided guidance indicating the circumstances in which it might seek to exercise its authority under section 502(a)(9), that is, when will the Secretary take action for breaches of fiduciary duty under section 502(a)(9) and what type of remedy will the Secretary seek. One dissenting vote believed that because section 502(a)(9) was a civil enforcement provision, the Department should not issue guidance, but should have flexibility on how and when it would use the provision.

The Council noted that even if a fiduciary breach has been established in connection with the purchasing of annuities, there is very little guidance in case law or elsewhere concerning what remedies are appropriate for such a breach. Given that "appropriate relief" and "security bond" are undefined terms in the statute, the Secretary has the authority to provide guidance to further define and elucidate these statutory terms. The Department could issue guidance defining what "appropriate relief" might mean in various fiduciary breach scenarios involving annuity purchasing, including defining circumstances under which the issuance of a security bond may be appropriate. For these reasons, the Council recommends that the Department should consider elaborating on these issues under section 502(a)(9) of ERISA.

D. Education and Outreach to Plan Sponsors

During the testimony, a number of issues were discussed that lead to the Council deciding to recommend that DOL provide education and outreach to plan sponsors. Much of the testimony from the plan sponsors and benefit consultants focused on the use of lump sum distributions and annuity purchases; there was somewhat limited testimony on the use of other strategies to de-risk. Because the Council heard that plan sponsors were concerned about volatility, the Council voted, with one dissent, to recommend that the Department provide education and outreach on the range of all available options including lump sum distributions and buy-outs. The dissent contended that there was no need for the Department to provide information about lump sums and annuity buy-outs and that this could be construed as an endorsement. The rationale for this recommendation was that the Council is concerned that small to medium size plan sponsors might not realize that there are options other than lump sum distributions to mitigate the risk in their defined benefit pension plans.

The testimony predominately indicated that while the decision to de-risk and offer lump sum options and buy-outs is a settlor function, the implementation of such a decision is a fiduciary one. However, there are some areas where education and outreach on whether a particular action is a settlor function would be helpful, as would guidance on fiduciary implementation issues. It would enable plan sponsors and plans to ensure that they are cognizant of their rights and responsibilities.

Other issues upon which the Council spent considerable time were the distinctions among disclosures, education and advice. If participants decide to choose a lump sum option, they must decide how they will handle the distribution. For example, participants need to decide the following: will they roll the distribution over to an individual retirement account; what are the personal tax consequences of the decision; if they roll it over, how will they invest it; how will they decide to draw down the lump sum so they do not outspend it? Many plan sponsors provide disclosures, call center services, and other "advisors." Although the Council recognizes that some of these issues may be encompassed in the Department's proposed changes to the regulation on the definition of fiduciary and accompanying guidance, the Council believes that it would be helpful for the plan to know where the line is between advice and mere education, and thus suggest that DOL provide education and outreach on these issues to plan sponsors and participants.

E. Collection of De-risking Data

The Council believes that it may be helpful to collect data on de-risking transactions to assist the Department in identifying any trends in regard to these transactions. This need became particularly evident as the Council found it difficult to obtain accurate information about the number and method of de-risking transactions for specific time periods.

The Department could use this information in various ways. For example:

- Substantial lump sum activity might underscore the importance of lump sum disclosures, and any pending lump sum disclosure guidance (or it may merely reflect dynamics within certain employers);
- Substantial annuity purchases from the same insurer(s) might indicate emerging market limitations (or it may merely reflect successful marketing and/or competitiveness).

Additional data might form the foundation for assessing the level of de-risking activity and identifying potential areas of concern. Generally, enhancing transparency and accountability is beneficial for the retirement system, as a whole, and to participants, in particular.

Although the Form 5500 could be used to collect this information, as it is the primary source of information concerning the operation, funding, assets, and investments of pension plans, it is not the only method for collection of information. The Council thought it appropriate to have DOL determine the best method of collection, as well as the specific pieces of information to be collected depending on how the Department might use the information. In addition, the collection vehicle could be coordinated with the Internal Revenue Service (IRS) and the Pension Benefit Guaranty Corporation (PBGC), keeping in mind its potential use by other federal agencies, Congress, and the private sector in assessing employee benefit, tax, and economic trends and policies. Moreover, such coordination might be necessary if the information is collected on Form 5500, which is an interagency form.

F. Intergovernmental Cooperation

Some de-risking transaction issues overlap among the three agencies responsible for overseeing ERISA-sponsored retirement plans. Other issues are discrete to a specific agency, but might impact the decisions which plan sponsors, plans, insurers and participants make. Regardless of the issues, coordination among the agencies to provide a holistic response would be most beneficial to the involved parties.

The Council had significant discussion concerning the potential tax implications of accepting a lump sum distribution when participants were already in pay status. The issues included whether the lump sum could be rolled over without immediate payment of taxes, and if an annuity distribution began before age 55, whether the 10% penalty must be paid on the lump sum distribution. Although the Council recognizes that these questions are not within the Department's jurisdiction, the Council believes that this information is necessary in order for a participant to make an informed decision. If, for example, a participant who began receiving monthly income payments from a pension plan at age 54, and then at age 60 was offered a $500,000 lump sum distribution, would not want to pay $50,000 in a penalty to the Internal Revenue Service, if that was required under the Code.

Another Treasury/IRS issue upon which the Council spent a considerable amount of time was the effect of the 80% funding rule on de-risking transactions. In particular, some Council members were concerned that the plan would end up funded below the 80% requirement after de-risking transactions. That requirement prohibits an amendment to a defined benefit plan which increases the plan's liabilities due to the establishment of a new benefit (which a lump sum distribution to deferred vested terminated participants frequently is) if the adjusted funding target attainment percentage is less than 80 percent or would be less than 80 percent, taking into account the amendment. ERISA §§ 206(g)(2)(A) & 303(d)(2), 29 U.S.C. §§ 1056(g)(2) & 1083(d)(2). Some Council members pointed out that a plan usually makes additional contributions before a de-risking transaction to ensure that the plan remains above the 80% funding mark.

A few Council members also raised concerns about the applicability of nondiscrimination rules and about plan qualification under Code § 415 (individual limits on qualified plan benefits) and Code § 404 (limits on employer deductions).

The Council commends DOL for its participant education efforts surrounding lifetime income stream versus lump sum distributions in the defined contribution plan context. The Council believes that de-risking transactions, which also offer the choice of a lump sum distribution, underscore the necessity for the Department's continued work in this area. The Council also recognizes that the PBGC and the Treasury/IRS have been working to make the choice of a lifetime income stream easier to make. The Council believes that continued coordination among all of these governmental agencies could be fruitful in increasing participants' understanding of the benefits of a lifetime income stream.

VI. Concluding Observations

After receiving testimony from diverse stakeholders and extensive and spirited deliberations, the Council attempted to balance the voluntary nature of the pension system with the need for participant protections where the plan sponsor has decided to transfer risk to the participants and/or insurers.

The Council believes that clarification of the scope of IB 95-1 to include de-risking activity outside the scope of plan termination would be beneficial to plan sponsors and participants. The Council also recognized the importance of balancing competing considerations such as the speed of providing guidance and the importance of public input. For example, discussion noted that spirited public dialog regarding any proposed safe harbors, within the scope of the Interpretive Bulletin, would contribute further to the proper implementation of any new standards the Department of Labor was considering establishing.

Similar to previous Councils, this Council believes that the prospect of a participant not maintaining a lifetime income stream as part of his or her retirement plan is a serious issue. Participants need to understand and make informed decisions regarding a lump sum distribution, including the fact that participants might outlive their assets. On the other hand, for some participants, lump sums may be an appropriate option. One obvious example of this is if they have a terminal illness. Consequently, providing clear, accurate and comprehensive disclosures to participants on the choice of receiving a lump sum distribution versus an annuity (whether from the plan or from a private insurer) is crucial in order for participants to make an informed choice for their retirement security.

Many members of the Council agreed with PBGC Director Josh Gotbaum's assessment that for a good portion of participants, lump sum distributions are not in their best interests. Although the Council was split on the precise scope of such a conclusion, it did suggest that a future Advisory Council might consider examining the reasons participants choose lump sum distributions; the steps that could be taken to increase participants' understanding of longevity, investment and interest risks for both defined benefit and defined contribution plans; and policies that could reduce the incentives that cause them to choose lump sum distributions over annuities. This would clearly fit into the Department's work on lifetime income streams and continue the work other Advisory Councils have completed, including last year's report by the Council, "Examining Income Replacement."

The additional recommendations offered by the Council further underscore the opportunities to provide further participant protections as well as further clarity in the administration of existing ERISA protections.

Finally, given the overlapping jurisdiction of governmental agencies on these issues, the Council suggests that DOL forward this report to the PBGC and the IRS/Treasury for their review in considering whether it necessary for them to take any action on de-risking transactions. One particular concern the Council had was the potential tax implications for the plan and/or for the participant of the election of a lump sum distribution when the participant is in pay status. Clarification of this and other potential tax implications would be helpful to both plan sponsors and participants.

The Council's modest efforts here only highlight the importance of continuing conversations between stakeholders concerning lifetime income streams versus lump sum distributions and the impact on participants' retirement security and the American economy. Consequently, the Council suggests that these issues remain ripe for review by the Council in subsequent years to survey the state of the industry, the response of stakeholders in the benefits community, and current problems.

The Council respectfully commends its recommendations to the Secretary, which will bolster his efforts to promote and protect benefit plan security for participants and beneficiaries. Beyond the utility of the recommendations, the Council hopes that its exploration of the issues surrounding de-risking will be of interest and assistance to all stakeholders.

ACKNOWLEDGEMENTS

The Council recognizes the following individuals and organizations who contributed greatly to the Council's deliberations and final report. Notwithstanding their contributions, any errors in the report rest with the Council alone.

Larry Good, EBSA, DOL
DiWeena Streater, EBSA, DOL
Witnesses from June 5, 2013
Joe Canary, EBSA, DOL
Robert Newman, Covington & Burling LLP

Steve Keating, Penbridge Advisors

Evan Inglis, Vanguard

Craig Rosenthal, Mercer, on behalf of American Benefits Council

John Ferreira, Morgan, Lewis & Bockius LLP

Ilana Boivie, Communications Workers of America

Jack Cohen, Association of BellTel Retirees

Witnesses from August 29, 2013

Bill Kadereit, National Retiree Legislative Network

Karen Friedman, Pension Rights Center

David Certner, AARP

Karin Feldman, AFL-CIO

Brendan Maher, University of Connecticut School of Law

Norman Stein, Drexel University, Earle Mack School of Law

Josh Gotbaum, Pension Benefit Guaranty Corporation

Philip Barlow, District of Columbia. Department. of Insurance, Securities and Banking

Peter Gallanis, National Organization of Life and Health Guaranty Associations

Preston Crabill, General Motors

Phil Waldeck, Prudential Financial, Inc.

Naomi Zwerling, MetLife, Inc.

Witnesses from September 23, 2013

Lynn Dudley, American Benefits Council

Kent A. Mason, Davis & Harman, LLP, on behalf of American Benefits Council

*Witnesses from November 4, 2013*_Karin Feldman, AFL-CIO

INDEX

A

B

C

D

E

J

L

M

N